Breaking Up With The Enemy

How to Defeat the Devil's Deceit and Reclaim Peace, Hope, and Joy

by Mike Manuel

Mike Manuel

© 2024 MOTA Publishing

www.MotaMinistries.com

Introduction 5

Chapter 1
The Unseen Battle 7

Chapter 2
The Power of Your Agreement 21

Chapter 3
Breaking Strongholds 35

Chapter 4
Robed In Righteousness 47

Chapter 5
Breaking Up With Unholy Soul Ties 61

Chapter 6
Breaking Up With Guilt, Shame, and
Condemnation 71

Chapter 7
Breaking Up With the Orphan Spirit 83

Chapter 8
Breaking Up With Unforgiveness 95

Chapter 9
Breaking Up With Self-Pity 109

Chapter 10
Breaking Up With The Religious Spirit 121

Chapter 11
Closing Commonly-Opened Doors 131

Chapter 12
Hearing From Jesus 145

Epilogue
Living in Freedom 149

Mike Manuel

Introduction

Have you ever felt like peace, hope, and joy are out of reach? Do you wonder why, despite your faith, you still struggle to experience the abundant life promised in God's Word? You're not alone.

In *Breaking Up With The Enemy: How To Defeat The Devil's Deceit and Reclaim Peace, Hope, and Joy*, I reveal the reason behind this all-too-common struggle: entanglement with the enemy. Satan and his army of fallen angels are constantly working to steal your peace, hope, and joy, replacing them with chaos, hopelessness, and despair. The worst part? Most people are unaware of how they unwittingly allow this to happen.

But there is hope. In this transformative book, you'll discover the true nature of the enemy's operations, the limits of his power, and, most importantly, how to break free from his grasp once and for all. You'll learn to demolish the strongholds in your life and tap into the supernatural power and authority that Jesus has given you.

This is not another self-help book. *Breaking Up With The Enemy* is a guide to embracing the life you were meant to live – a life filled with the peace, hope, and joy that come from walking in the power and freedom of Jesus.

In the first three chapters, we'll explore how we all, at some point, find ourselves in a toxic relationship with the enemy. Don't worry – you're not alone, and it's never too late to break free.

The fundamental transformation begins in the fourth chapter. You'll learn to recognize the enemy's lies and cut all ties with him, legally and permanently removing him from your life. As you embark on this journey, you'll feel the weight of anxiety, chaos, and despair lifting, replaced by a newfound sense of peace and joy. Hope will dawn in your life, perhaps for the first time.

These aren't empty promises but the real-life experiences of thousands of people like you who have emerged victorious through this process.

So, are you ready to break up with the enemy and embrace the abundant life that awaits you? Let's get started!

Chapter 1

The Unseen Battle

As you walk out your journey of faith, you must understand the reality of the spiritual battles we face daily. I know it can be unsettling to acknowledge, but the truth is that we have a very real enemy who is relentless in his pursuit to steal, kill, and destroy everything good in our lives.[1] Not only does he steal from us, but he also brings in a load of anxiety, chaos, fear, and despair and dumps it right in the pit of our emotions. This enemy is not flesh and blood but rather the spiritual forces of evil – Satan himself and his army of fallen angels. [2]

The most disturbing news is not that we have an enemy but that we've granted him access to our lives and allowed him to steal our peace, hope, and joy. Wait, what? We've granted the devil access? Is that even biblical? Yes, it's biblical, and many people have opened doors to their spiritual enemy and don't even know it. I've done it, and you probably have, too.

Many of you reading this book may have found peace, hope, and joy somewhat elusive. Maybe you're dealing with anxiety, chaos, or despair in your life right now. Perhaps you don't even feel any emotion. You've just gone numb and can't feel anything—good or bad.

The bad news is that the enemy most likely causes these negative emotions in your life. The good news is that the enemy most likely causes these negative emotions in your life. Yes, you read this correctly. The bad news is also the good news. The news is bad because the devil and his army of fallen angels (Jesus calls them demons[3]) have been able to affect your life negatively. However, it's also good news because Jesus gave all his followers power and authority to defeat and disable all the work of the enemy in our lives. [4]

As you read this book and follow the instructions, you'll learn how to eradicate the destructive work of the enemy in your life by using the power and authority Jesus gave you.

How It All Began

The Bible is crystal clear about the existence of the demonic realm. The Old Testament books of Ezekiel and Isaiah and the New Testament book of

Revelation give us a glimpse into how this dark kingdom came into being.

Here's the backstory in a nutshell: Satan, originally called Lucifer (which means "light-bearer"), was once a beautiful angel who had the prestigious role of being the worship leader in heaven. Can you imagine that? The one who now opposes God was once in charge of worshipping Him! But as the old saying goes, pride comes before a fall. Lucifer allowed his God-given beauty and position to go to his head, and he began to crave the worship and adoration that belonged to God alone.

In a shocking display of rebellion, Lucifer convinced a third of the angels to join him in an uprising against their Creator.[5] As a result, God cast them out of heaven, and they were hurled down to the earth. From that moment on, Lucifer became known as Satan, which means "adversary." He and his fallen angels, now demons, became the sworn enemies of God and His people.

Their mission? To oppose God's purposes and lead humanity astray at every turn. And while Satan is not omnipresent, omniscient, or omnipotent like our heavenly Father, he is still a formidable foe. As the commander-in-chief of this dark kingdom, he deploys his demons to carry out his schemes and wreak havoc in the lives of God's children.

But I have good news! If you have put your faith in Jesus Christ, you have no reason to cower in fear of Satan or his minions. The moment you accepted Jesus as your Savior, your eternal destiny was sealed, and no demon can ever snatch you out of God's hand.[6] Your salvation is secure! However, this doesn't mean the enemy will wave a white flag and leave you alone. Oh no. In fact, he will stop at nothing to make your life on this earth as miserable as possible.

You see, Satan hates you with a burning passion because you bear the image of God and are deeply loved by Him. It infuriates him that he can't touch your spirit, which has been made righteous through faith in Christ. So, instead, he zeroes in on your soul – your mind, will, and emotions. This is why the Apostle Peter urges us to "be sober-minded" and "watchful" because our "adversary, the devil, prowls around like a roaring lion, seeking someone to devour."[7]

The Enemy's Tactics

So, what does this look like in our day-to-day lives? How does Satan attack our souls? Well, one of his go-to tactics is deception. Jesus called him "a liar and the father of lies."[8] From the very beginning, Satan's modus operandi has been to twist God's words and sow seeds of doubt in our minds. He whispers accusations, telling us we're not good enough, that God couldn't possibly love someone with a past like ours, and that our sins are too great to be forgiven. He magnifies our fears and insecurities, tempting us to find comfort and validation in all the wrong places.

If we're not careful, these lies can take root in our souls, creating strongholds of unbelief, bitterness, fear, and addiction. We may find ourselves plagued by anxiety, depression, or even physical ailments that seem to have no apparent medical explanation. These are often telltale signs that a spiritual battle is raging for our minds and emotions.

But here's the thing—you are not defenseless in this fight! The moment you surrendered your life to Jesus, you were forgiven and cleansed and given a new identity and authority in Christ. You are now a child of the Most High God, and He has given you authority to "tread on serpents and scorpions," representing the demonic forces and "over all the power of the enemy." [9]

You Are NOT Demon-Possessed

Demon possession is a real thing, but if you are a true believer in Jesus Christ, it's impossible for you to be possessed by a demon as defined by our modern use of the term *possession*. Possession in our contemporary language implies control, and if you're a blood-bought follower of Christ, no demon can control you. The word *possessed* is used several times in the New Testament as it relates to demonic activity, and it's interesting to note that the main Greek root word for possess means *to hold on to, to hold a view, or to experience a state or condition*.[10] So what is translated as demonic possession in our modern language could, in many cases, be more accurately referred to as demonic oppression. According to the dictionary, the word *oppressed* means *to be burdened cruelly or unjustly*. In other words, oppression weighs us down and is unfair.

So, while demon possession in the traditional sense is relatively rare, demon oppression is not.

You don't have to look very hard to see the effects of demonic oppression all around us. You might not even have to look further than your own life. The primary way demons oppress us is by speaking to our conscience and influencing us to believe a lie. We act on what we believe; if we believe a lie, we'll live it out as if it were the truth.

Engaging in Spiritual Warfare

How do we engage in this spiritual warfare and resist the devil's schemes? It starts with knowing the truth about who you are in Christ and renewing your mind with the promises found in God's Word.[11] When you fill your heart and mind with Scripture, meditating on God's faithfulness and goodness, you become less vulnerable to the enemy's lies. You learn to take every thought captive and make it obedient to Christ. [12]

Renewing your mind is not a one-time event but a daily discipline. It requires consistency and intentionality, but the more you immerse yourself in God's truth, the more quickly you'll recognize the enemy's deceptions. You'll begin to see yourself through God's eyes—as a child He loves, chosen and set apart for His purposes. You'll find your confidence growing, not in your strength or abilities but in God's unshakable promises.

Another powerful weapon in our arsenal is prayer. When you spend time in God's presence, pouring out your heart to Him and listening for His voice, you open yourself up to receive His strength, wisdom, and guidance for your battles. The Apostle Paul urges us to pray at all times in the Spirit, staying alert and persistent in our requests. [13]

There is no magic formula or particular set of words—it's all about coming before God with a humble, faith-filled heart and boldly approaching His throne of grace to receive the help we need.[14] As you cultivate a lifestyle of prayer, you'll find yourself growing more sensitive to the Holy Spirit's leading. You'll learn to discern His voice above the world's clamor and the enemy's lies. And you'll experience a more significant measure of peace and authority, even during life's storms.

Engaging in spiritual warfare sometimes means making tough choices to break free from the enemy's influence. It may involve confessing and repenting of sins that have given Satan a foothold in your life, such as unforgiveness, pride, or sexual immorality. It may mean setting boundaries in your relationships or cutting ties with negative influences that are pulling you away from God's best for you.

None of this is easy, but as you submit yourself to God and resist the devil, Scripture promises that he will flee from you.[15] It's important to remember that this is not a one-time event but an ongoing process. As you continue to walk in obedience and surrender to God, the enemy's grip on your life will loosen. You'll experience a newfound freedom and joy from living in alignment with God's will.

Understanding Our Make-Up

To understand how the enemy can oppress us, we need to understand our makeup. The Bible tells us we're three-part beings—body, soul, and spirit. These three parts of us, even though they're separate, work so closely together that it seems to us like there's only one big part. But to understand how the demonic realm can oppress us, we'll need to take a closer look at the three parts that make us one human being.

Let's start by looking at how our soul and body work together. Our soul is our mind, our will, our intellect, our personality, and the seat of our emotions. Our soul is who we really are, and it will live forever in one of two places - either with Jesus or without him. Our body, which is made up mostly of carbon and water, is the temporary housing for our permanent soul. Our brain, part of our temporary body, is an information processor that our soul accesses to rationalize, think and act. Our soul, which is not physical, experiences this physical world through our physical body.

For example, if I smell a particular smell, my brain can't tell how I *feel* about what I'm smelling; it can only tell me *what* I'm smelling. How I feel about what I'm smelling comes from my soul, not my brain, because my emotions (feelings) come from my soul and not my brain. A smell is a group of molecules that enter my nose and come in contact with olfactory nerves. The olfactory nerves then send an electrical impulse to my brain (information processor), and after a few quick calculations, my brain makes a determination of what the smell is. My soul then accesses the brain and decides how that smell makes me feel (an emotion). As a point of interest, scientists say that smells evoke more emotions in us than any of the other four senses.

I grew up on a farm, and as an adult, I farmed for several years before becoming a pastor. For me, one of the best smells is freshly tilled soil. You gardeners know precisely what I'm talking about! Nowadays, when I smell newly tilled soil, I'm overwhelmed with warm memories of my childhood, feeling a love for the land and thinking back to simpler days. It feels good. When I smell Juicy Fruit gum, I think of my grandma and how much she loved me and how much I miss her. When I smell the antiseptic smell of a hospital, my stomach begins to churn as I recount the days I spent at the hospital visiting my younger brother, who died of cancer at age 30.

But just as our body can affect our soul, our soul can, in turn, affect our body. Medical experts say that over 80% of our illnesses are brought on by stress. Since stress is an emotion and emotions come from the soul, we can connect the dots and say that our soul affects our body. This fact will be necessary to remember later as we discuss how the enemy's attack on our soul can adversely affect our physical body.

Now, it's time to talk about our spirit. Rather than say we have a spirit, it's more accurate to say we *are* a spirit. The Bible says we are made in

God's image and that God is spirit. Our spirit is the "God-conscious" part of us, which sets us apart from the rest of God's creation. Just as our soul experiences the natural world through our physical body, our soul can also experience the spiritual realm through our spirit.

Jesus said that we, his sheep, hear and know his voice.[16] I know very few people who have heard the audible voice of Jesus through their physical ears, but I know countless many, myself included, who have heard his voice through their spirit. I also know very few people who have seen Jesus with their physical eyes, yet many others and I have seen Jesus in the spiritual realm. If that sounds like heresy, Jesus told us he would show himself to those who love him.[17] The bottom line is that the supernatural realm is accessible through our spirit, just as the natural world is accessible through our body.

The Enemy's Access Point

When you receive Jesus as your Savior and trust in his sacrifice on the cross as full payment for your sins, the Bible says you are made perfectly righteous in the eyes of God the Father. What's made perfect is your spirit, not your soul.

Your spirit is made perfect instantly when you put your trust in Jesus. It's called justification. Your soul, however, is a work in progress, and that process is called sanctification.

The enemy has no legal right and no power to attack the spirit of a believer because that spirit has been made perfect by the blood of Jesus, and nothing can spoil that perfection. Our soul, however, is imperfect, and that's where the enemy attacks. As we learned earlier in this chapter, the Bible warns us that our enemy, the devil, prowls around like a roaring lion looking for someone to devour.

But this concept of the devil attacking us raises an important question that must be answered. If the death and resurrection of Jesus defeated Satan, then how does he have the right to attack us? That's a great question because it's an absolute biblical truth that Jesus defeated the enemy on the cross[18], yet we're warned to be vigilant against his attacks. How can both of those be true at the same time? To find the answer to this question, please turn to the next chapter. The answer may surprise you.

Mike Manuel

---

[1] John 10:10
[2] Ephesians 6:12
[3] Matthew 10:8
[4] Luke 10:19
[5] Isaiah 14:12-15   Ezekiel 28:12-19   Revelation 12:4
[6] John 10:28-29
[7] 1 Peter 5:8
[8] John 8:44
[9] Luke 10:19
[10] Goodrick-Kohlenberger #2400
[11] Romans 12:2
[12] 2 Corinthians 10:5
[13] Ephesians 6:18
[14] Hebrews 4:16
[15] James 4:7
[16] John 10:3-4
[17] John 14:21
[18] Colossians 2:15

Chapter 2

The Power of Your Agreement

The Gift of Authority

It all started in the Garden of Eden. When God created Adam and Eve, the first humans, He gave them an incredible gift - power and authority on the earth.[1] Make no mistake: God is entirely sovereign and rules over all creation. But in His infinite wisdom and grace, God chose to entrust humanity with meaningful responsibility. He gave you and me the extraordinary privilege of being his representatives and agents in advancing His kingdom on earth.

Can you imagine the magnitude of this gift? The Creator of the universe, the all-powerful, all-knowing, all-loving God, has chosen to partner with us in bringing His goodness and righteousness to bear on this world. He could have kept all authority for himself. He could have micromanaged every detail. But instead, in an astonishing act of love and trust, He has given us a role to play, a sacred stewardship.

The Tragic Consequences of Rebellion

Sadly, as we read in Genesis, Adam and Eve were careless with their God-given authority. They used their free will to agree with Satan's crafty temptation to eat the forbidden fruit. When they did, it was like opening Pandora's box, unleashing evil, sin, and destruction into the world. Suddenly, the earth was no longer a perfect paradise.

I don't believe that this turn of events took God by surprise. God is all-knowing. He was well aware that in giving humans free will, we wouldn't always choose to follow His perfect ways. This raises an interesting question I've wrestled with over the years: Is God's will always done? Is everything that happens on earth a reflection of what God desires?

Years ago, I would have responded to that question with an emphatic "Yes, of course! God is in complete control." But that answer wasn't based on a careful study of Scripture. It was more what I wanted to be true because the alternative—the idea that God's will might sometimes not be done—felt too uncomfortable, too threatening to my understanding of who God is.

But as I've dug deeper into God's Word, I've recognized that the Bible reveals a more nuanced reality. The Bible clearly states that God is "not willing that any should perish, but that all should come to repentance."[2] In other words, it is decidedly not God's will for anyone to die without receiving the gift of salvation and end up eternally separated from Him in hell. Yet the heartbreaking truth is that unsaved people are dying and going to hell every day.

Or consider the horrific evil in our world - child abuse, human trafficking, rape, murder. Could we say that such grievous sins are God's will? Scripture assures us that God is light; in Him there is no darkness at all.[3] Evil is never God's desire or his doing. Instead, it is the tragic consequence of us humans using our free will to disagree with God and go our own way.

Please understand that I am not implying that humans are more powerful than God or that we can ultimately thwart His sovereign plans. God is omnipotent (all-powerful). Nothing and no one can overcome Him. And yet, because God is love,[4] He has given us the gift of free will. We can agree with God and His ways or go rogue and unwittingly align ourselves with the enemy's schemes. And that, my friend, is where things get crucial—the nitty-gritty of this spiritual life.

Coming into Agreement with the Enemy

Every time you and I disagree with God, whether knowingly or unknowingly, we are giving our consent to the devil. We're signing off on his right to meddle in our lives and bring harm. The only power the devil has in your life comes from your agreement.

I can imagine what you might think because I've felt it myself: "I would never disagree with God!" But the truth is, we do this far more often than we realize. In the seemingly small moments, the subtle choices, we can find ourselves aligning with the enemy's agenda rather than God's.

Say you wake up one morning, and when your feet hit the floor, your thoughts start down a negative path: "Ugh, today is going to be the worst. I just know it. My boss is going to be in a foul mood, I'll probably catch that nasty cold that's been going around the office, and I'll be drowning in projects that I can never get done. Yep, it's going to be a rotten day."

Here's the problem: those words coming out of your mouth directly contradict what God says about your day. The Bible says, "This is the day that the Lord has made; let us rejoice and be glad in it."[5] So when you prophesy doom and gloom over your day, you're agreeing with the enemy. You're empowering Satan's agenda to "steal, kill, and destroy."[6]

But what if you made a different choice? What if, even though you may not feel like it, you choose to agree with God's Word? Imagine starting your morning like this: "Lord, thank you for this brand new day. Even though I don't know everything it holds, I trust that You are good and have good plans for me. I rejoice, knowing that Your mercies are fresh every morning. Great is Your faithfulness! Help me to see Your hand at work in my life today."

You've pulled the rug out from under the devil's schemes in this scenario. Not only that, but you've released the power of the Holy Spirit to work on your behalf, bringing supernatural favor, strength, and wisdom to your day. That, my friend, is the power of prayer. When you and I speak God's Word over our lives, we wield a mighty weapon.

Did you know two spiritual kingdoms are eavesdropping whenever you open your mouth, ready to run with what you say? The kingdom of light and the kingdom of darkness. The Holy Spirit is poised to bring to pass every word you speak that aligns with God's Word and his will.[7] At the same time, demonic forces are ready to pounce on every idle word, every fearful whisper, every bitter complaint. That's why Jesus warned us to be careful about what we say. [8]

I used to read Proverbs 18:21 and quickly skim over it: "Death and life are in the power of the tongue, and those who love it will eat its fruits." I'd take away the simple lesson of saying nice things and avoiding saying mean things. It's not bad advice, but that verse means so much more. It tells us that our words are a matter of light or darkness in the most literal sense.

When you speak, you are either commissioning angels or demons to get to work, inviting heaven's intervention or hell's interference. I don't know about you, but that stops me in my tracks. It makes me want to really think before I speak.

Just imagine the impact we could have if we truly grasped the weight of our words. What if we intentionally spoke life, blessing, and truth over ourselves and others? What if we declared God's promises over them instead of complaining about our circumstances? Instead of tearing others down with criticism, what if we built them up with encouragement? We would see a radical shift, not only in our own lives but in the world around us.

Empowering the Jailer

So, what does it look like to give the enemy a foothold in your life through an ungodly agreement? First, it's essential to understand that as a believer in Christ, your spirit has been made new. The Bible says you are a "new creation."[9] Your born-again spirit is untouchable to the forces of darkness because it is sealed by the Holy Spirit.[10]

But your soul - that's another matter. Your soul is made up of your mind, your will, and your emotions. And that's the entry point the devil is looking for. When you come into agreement with Satan's lies and ways of thinking, you open a door in your soul for his oppression.

Mike Manuel

Oppression - that's a keyword I want you to understand. As a child of God, you can never be possessed by a demon. You belong to Jesus; Satan can't own you. But he can oppress you. He can come in and influence your thoughts, stir up ungodly feelings, and pressure your will. That's what the Bible means when discussing the devil's "schemes" and "fiery darts." [11]

Frankly, from my experience in dealing with spiritual warfare, the enemy isn't all that creative or original. He tends to use the same predictable tactics: fear, doubt, shame, anxiety, confusion, bitterness, jealousy, greed, and offense, to name a few. But here's what I want you to get: he can't just jump in and start messing with your mind and heart on a whim. Somewhere, somehow, he needs your agreement.

Maybe you've felt a heaviness, a dark cloud hanging over you that you can't seem to shake. Or you find yourself wrestling with obsessive thoughts that are the opposite of God's Word. You could be dealing with irrational fears, overwhelming loneliness, or uncontrollable anger. I can almost guarantee that if you trace it back, you'll find a point of agreement with the enemy. Somewhere in your words or actions, you gave him consent to harass you, and you were probably unaware of it.

And it's not always in the obvious areas. Sometimes, it's in the subtle lies we believe about ourselves, the self-talk that contradicts what God says about us. Thoughts like: "I'm not good enough. I'll never measure up. I'm too far gone for God to fix me." Those thoughts are not from God. They're the whispers of the enemy, seeking to keep you in bondage to insecurity and inadequacy.

Or maybe it's in the offense and unforgiveness we harbor towards others. When someone hurts us, our flesh wants to hold onto that pain, nurse the wound, and justify our right to be bitter. But scripture is clear: unforgiveness is a dangerous open door to the devil's oppression.

Jesus gives us a powerful illustration of how we give legal consent to the enemy. In Matthew 18, he tells the story of a servant who owed an enormous debt he could never repay in a million lifetimes. The king who owned the debt chose to have mercy and completely forgive the servant. But then that same servant found a man who owed him a much smaller sum. Instead of extending the same mercy he had received, the servant had the man thrown into debtor's prison.

When the king heard about this, he was furious. He called the servant back and had him turned over to the jailer to be tortured until he could pay back all he owed—which was impossible. Then Jesus made this sobering statement: "So also my heavenly Father will do to every one of you if you do not forgive your brother from your heart."[12]

Okay, let's unpack this. God is not a jailer or a torturer. Every good and perfect gift comes from God,[13] and He doesn't change like shifting shadows. God is always good. He disciplines those he loves,[14] but He doesn't torture us.

So, who is the jailer and torturer in this story? It's the devil and his demonic army. When we refuse to forgive someone and hold onto bitterness and offense, we agree with the enemy. We may think we're punishing the person who hurt us, but in reality, we've just given Satan legal access to our lives as a jailer and torturer.

Forgiveness is not an option for followers of Christ. It's a command. God's Word tells us to forgive as the Lord forgave us.[15] So when we withhold forgiveness, we're living in disagreement with God. We're agreeing with Satan's way rather than God's way. And the result? The enemy gets to come in and oppress us, messing with our minds and emotions and stealing our peace and joy.

That's how the devil builds strongholds—fortified places in our thought lives where we disagree with God. He gains access through our agreement, and then he sets up camp. He starts feeding us his perspective until it feels like that's the only reality.

How to Fight This Battle

But here's the good news: you have the divine power to demolish strongholds![16] As you renounce your agreement with the enemy, repent for any way you've aligned yourself with his lies, and choose to forgive and bless even those who have hurt you - you close the door to the devil. You revoke his access. And as you fill your mind with God's Word and worship, as you agree with what God says about you and your situations, you create an atmosphere where the Holy Spirit can do His supernatural work in you.

This is how we fight our battles—not with fists or fury but in intimate prayer, passionate worship, and walking in our God-given authority. In this secret place of intimacy with God, we are strengthened and equipped to resist the devil and see him flee.[17] We find overcoming power as we abide in Christ and let His Word abide in us.[18]

Here's my challenge: start paying attention to what you agree with. Take every thought captive to obey Christ. When you find yourself starting to spiral into fear, anxiety, or negativity, stop and ask: "Is this thought in alignment with God's Word? Am I agreeing with God's truth or the devil's lies?"

And then choose to speak life. Declare God's promises over your circumstances. Prophesy His goodness and faithfulness over your future. Agree with His Word, even when your feelings are shouting the opposite.

As you do, the enemy's hold on your life will begin to break. You'll experience a newfound freedom and joy that can only come from aligning yourself with God's ways. And you'll start to see His kingdom come, and His will be done—in your life and in the world around you.

Don't underestimate the power of your agreement. Every thought you entertain, every word you speak, and every choice you make advances God's kingdom or gives ground to the enemy. Let's be intentional about aligning ourselves with heaven and resisting the devil. We'll see God's unshakeable victory manifested in our lives as we do.

In the next chapter, we'll see how our agreements with the enemy establish strongholds in our lives. We'll learn what a stronghold is and, more importantly, how to eliminate it.

---

[1] Genesis 1:28

[2] 2 Peter 3:9

[3] 1 John 1:5

[4] 1 John 4:8

[5] Psalm 118:24

[6] John 10:10

[7] John 14:13-14

[8] Matthew 12:36-37

[9] 2 Corinthians 5:17

[10] Ephesians 1:13

[11] Ephesians 6:11-16

[12] Matthew 18:2-35

[13] James 1:17

[14] Hebrews 12:6

[15] Colossians 3:13

[16] 2 Corinthians 10:4

Mike Manuel

---

[17] James 4:7

[18] John 15:7

Chapter 3

Breaking Strongholds

Stronghold is a term in the Bible; its literal meaning is a *well-fortified place, a fortress*. During biblical times, a stronghold was primarily constructed of rock and iron and was used either to keep bad people in (jail) or bad people out (a castle or fortress). You'll find the term *stronghold* used many times in the Old Testament, usually in the context of its literal meaning of a well-fortified building. However, stronghold is also used in the Old Testament as a metaphor for God's protection.

Interestingly, the word stronghold is only used once in the New Testament, in 2 Corinthians 10:4. In this instance, it's used as a metaphor to illustrate a type of prison that the enemy has established in our mind (soul) to oppress us and keep us from a closer relationship with God.

Many people are currently being held captive by a stronghold that has been established in their souls and oppresses them in the form of anxiety, fear, chaos, anger, addictions, despair, hopelessness, guilt, shame, condemnation, and the list goes on and on.

How Strongholds Are Established

How did these strongholds get established in us? As I pointed out in the previous chapter, it all starts when we knowingly or unknowingly agree with the enemy, which gives them legal access (an open door) to attack our souls. The first step in establishing a stronghold begins with a lie. Just like in the Garden of Eden, Satan uses his smooth-talking lies to get us to agree with him. Jesus didn't pull any punches when he came right out and called Satan a liar.[1] He is relentless in his barrage of lies:

"You've messed up one too many times. There's no hope for you."

"Things look really bad for you, and it's only going to get worse."

"Aren't you concerned about this? This is something you should be worried about."

"It would be easier for everyone around you to end it now."

"The only thing that will make you feel better is another drink."

"Everyone's talking about you, and it's not good."

And it goes on and on—day after day.

One of the biggest problems with the enemy's lies is that most people don't attribute them to the devil. They think it's their own mind thinking these things. When the devil speaks, he doesn't sound like a growling demon. He sounds like us. That's because he speaks to our soul, and when we listen to our soul, it sounds like us. One of the enemy's most effective schemes is to lie to you in your own voice.

It's important to know that the enemy's lies have no power until we begin to believe them. If and when we start to believe the lies of the enemy, the foundation of a stronghold begins to be built in us. We become a captive in our own mind. What's even more disturbing is that most people aren't even aware of what's happening. They know something's different because they feel certain unexplainable emotions and desires but don't know where it's coming from. So they trudge ahead, hoping that tomorrow will be better.

But here's a newsflash: Tomorrow won't be better until we deal with the underlying issue, which is the stronghold established in our soul. It's time to demolish some strongholds.

Demolishing Strongholds

We need to be rescued from our captivity in the strongholds of our lives. You'll be glad to know that God has spoken of this rescue many times in His Word. Although you can find the word *rescue* in your Bible, the word most applicable here is *deliver*. You'll find the word deliver numerous times in the Bible, which literally means to rescue.

Perhaps the most often cited verse in the Bible that includes the word deliver is found in the Lord's Prayer. In Matthew 6, the disciples ask Jesus how to pray, and he gladly obliges them. Remember, he's teaching believers how to pray. That's important because, in his prayer, Jesus teaches us to pray for the Father to deliver us from evil. A better translation of that verse uses the phrase *deliver us from the evil one*. Because the word deliver here literally means rescue, we could rephrase it to say "rescue us from the evil one." I don't think there should be any confusion over who Jesus is referring to as the "evil one," but there might be some confusion over what this phrase means. Again, remember that Jesus is teaching *believers* to pray.

One fundamental truth about believers is that they're going to heaven. They don't have to be rescued from hell because they already are! However, Jesus knew there would be times when we, as believers, inadvertently agree with the devil and get entangled in his schemes. He knew there may be times when we could find ourselves a captive in a stronghold. In those times, we need to be rescued (delivered).

So, how does God deliver us from demonic strongholds in our lives? The answer, while being relatively simple, is amazing nonetheless. He gives us (believers) power and authority to overcome all the enemy's power.[2] What's ironic about this is that our careless use of our God-given authority empowers the enemy to attack us in the first place! And now Jesus tells us we have the power and authority to send the enemy packing. Simply put, our authority lets the enemy in, and our authority can kick him out.

You may remember that in the first chapter of this book, I said there is good news and bad news.

The bad news is that most of our negative emotions are likely caused by the enemy. The good news is that most of our negative emotions are likely caused by the enemy. The bad news is also good news because if our problems come from the enemy, we can use our God-given power and authority to defeat the enemy and evict him.

I've seen people spend thousands of dollars hoping that a counselor or therapist can help them find some peace, hope, and joy in their lives when all they'd have to do is receive Jesus as their Savior and then exercise their authority over the enemy. I'm not saying that every problem in your life is demonically inspired, and I'm also not saying that counselors and therapists aren't sometimes necessary. I *am* saying that if we, as followers of Christ, would realize the power and authority over the enemy that Jesus has given us, we could get rid of most of our emotional baggage right now and start living a life full of peace, hope, and joy.

We can demolish strongholds in our lives through the power of Jesus and break free from the chaos, hopelessness, and despair that the enemy tries to dump into our lives.

The Power of Shalom

I'm not a scholar of the Hebrew language, which is the Old Testament's original language, but I appreciate its richness and the symbolic meaning of each letter of the Hebrew alphabet. As we transition in this book from discovering the problem to getting rid of it, I want to share some encouraging insight regarding the Hebrew word *shalom*.

In English, we translate the word shalom as peace. While shalom means peace, it has a much richer meaning. In addition to peace, the word shalom means wholeness, well-being, tranquility, prosperity, health, contentment, and rest. Sounds pretty good, doesn't it?

Here's where it gets interesting. The word shalom consists of four Hebrew letters. But Hebrew letters of the alphabet are more than just letters. Each letter has a meaning, and the design of each letter is a graphic illustration of the meaning behind each letter. Below is the word shalom in Hebrew:

Hebrew words are read from right to left, so the first letter of shalom is the letter on the right. The first letter, shin, represents teeth and means to destroy. The second letter, lamed, represents a staff (like a king would have) and represents authority. The third letter, vav, represents a coat hook and means to establish. The fourth letter, mem, represents water (like an ocean) but can also mean chaos (like a windy ocean). So, let's look at the individual meaning of each of these letters: Destroy - Authority - Establish - Chaos. You could say it this way: Shalom means *to destroy the authority that establishes chaos*.

Are you ready for some shalom? Are you ready to destroy the authority that establishes chaos in your life? Are you ready to break up with the enemy? If so, keep reading!

A Godly Divorce

For the past several years, I have conducted nearly one hundred seminars (more information at www.MikeManuel.faith) that cover many of the same topics as those addressed in this book. As we minister at these seminars, we often use the phrase "cast out" when taking authority over the enemy and kicking them out of peoples' lives. I never saw a problem with using this term because these are the exact words that Jesus uses in Matthew 10:8 when He tells us to "cast out demons."

Several years ago, two well-meaning believers who had attended one of my conferences approached me to voice their concern regarding using the term "cast out" when I was ministering to seminar participants. They felt like those words might be too strong and could make people feel like they were demon-possessed. I took their concerns seriously because the last thing I want is for people to think of spinning heads and green vomit!

So, I began to think of other words my ministry team and I could use other than "cast out" during our ministry time. For several days, I ran different ideas through my head, and I even consulted a thesaurus at one point! But then a still, small voice spoke to my heart and said, "Why don't you investigate why Jesus used those words?"

So I turned to Matthew 10:8 and dug into the Greek word translated into English as "cast out" or "drive out." As I studied, I quickly learned that the main Greek root word meant "to divorce" or "cut off." I remember thinking, "Wow! Jesus wants us to divorce the enemy!"

That shed a whole new light on things for me. While many people might be unsure of the meaning of "cast out," everyone is familiar with the word "divorce."

For several decades, country music artists have been singing about the pain of divorce. Although I've never personally gone through a divorce, many people who are close to me have, and I've seen the pain that it causes. And we know from the scriptures that God hates divorce. God doesn't hate people who have gone through a divorce - He hates the process and the pain. But there's a time when God loves divorce, and it's when we decide to break up with the enemy and divorce him. Cut him off. Finished. Cast out!

Use Your Authority

When we get married and sign the marriage license, we're signing an agreement that states we're one with our new spouse. It's considered a legal contract. When people get divorced, they ask the legal system to dissolve their agreement. It's much the same with the enemy. We got legally entangled with him through our agreement. But here's the good news: The Judge has already given you the authority to break that agreement!

So, how do we break our agreement(s) with the enemy? It's relatively easy and not all that complicated. You don't have to outpower the devil or outshout him; you simply and clearly speak your divorce decree in the name of Jesus.

When I use the word *speak*, I mean it literally, and here's why. As I stated in a previous chapter, the devil doesn't have the attributes of God. One attribute of God is that he is all-knowing (omniscient). That means he knows what we're thinking. That's why we can pray to God by just thinking. But Satan, although he knows quite a bit, is not all-knowing. He can't read our mind. So if we're going to rebuke Satan, we can't do it by just thinking it. We have to voice it to him. We have to vibrate our vocal cords and let the enemy know in no uncertain terms that we are using our authority in Jesus Christ to break all agreements we've made with him and that we're casting him out of our life. We're speaking our divorce decree to him.

And here's the best part: he has to leave. When you exercise your authority as a blood-bought child of God, the enemy must obey. They have no other option because they have been defeated on the cross of Christ. Who would have ever thought that divorce could be this easy?

When the enemy leaves, he has to take all his junk with him. All the chaos, all the confusion, all the anxiety, all the fear, all the anger, all the hopelessness, all the despair. Whatever he brought in he has to take out. And all this time, you thought that junk was yours!

In the next chapter, you'll learn the first and most crucial step in breaking up with the enemy.

---

[1] John 8:44

[2] Luke 10:19

Chapter 4

Robed In Righteousness

According to the most recent Gallup Poll, 67% of Americans believe in heaven. If you were to ask them how to get to heaven, my guess is that the majority would say something like, "Just try to be a good person." As a pastor, I've worked with countless individuals who believe their goodness is the key to their admittance into heaven. They imagine a cosmic scoreboard, a tally of good deeds and bad, desperately hoping that they'll somehow make the cut.

But how good is good enough? Is 51% good enough? 75% good? 90% good? Can anyone be certain where the dividing line lies between heaven and hell?

What if I told you the Bible offers a definitive answer to this age-old question? What if the standard for entry into heaven is not some vague, shifting goal but a clear and uncompromising benchmark?

Brace yourself for the truth, which is as sobering as it is liberating.

The Impossible Standard

Let's cut to the chase: the requirement for entrance into heaven is not 51%, 75%, or even 90% goodness. No, the Bible sets the bar much, much higher.

Jesus reveals the standard as quoted in the Bible. "Be perfect, therefore, as your heavenly Father is perfect." [1]

Let that sink in for a moment. Perfection. Complete, unblemished righteousness. A flawless record of thought, word, and deed. 100% righteousness.

It's a sobering standard. If we're honest with ourselves, we must admit that it's an utterly impossible benchmark to reach. As the prophet Isaiah declared, "All of us have become like one who is unclean, and all our righteous acts are like filthy rags." [2]

The uncomfortable truth is that we are all once stained by sin. We all fall short of God's standard for righteousness.[3] From the moment we drew our first breath, we were tainted by the corruption that has plagued humanity since the fall.

The apostle Paul bluntly states in Romans 3:10, "There is no one righteous, not even one." This is a devastating indictment, a death knell for any hope of earning our way into heaven.

So, where does that leave us? If the entry requirement is 100% perfection, and we are hopelessly mired in imperfection, what chance do we have of gaining admission to eternity?

The Great Exchange

What if I told you that there is a way - a divinely ordained path - for us to be counted as perfect in God's sight despite our innate sinfulness? What if there was a means by which our filthy rags could be exchanged for a spotless robe of righteousness?

This, my friend, is the essence of the gospel, the heart of the good news that can transform lives for all eternity. We could call it "the great exchange," a transaction so audacious and undeserved that it can only be attributed to God's boundless grace.

At the center of this exchange stands a figure like no other: Jesus Christ, the eternal Son of God. Though fully divine, He willingly set aside His heavenly privileges to take on human flesh and live among us.

But Jesus was no ordinary man. He was the spotless Lamb of God, the only human being to walk this earth in perfect obedience to the Father. There was no sin, no shadow of turning, no hint of imperfection in Him.

And yet, in a stunning display of sacrificial love, Jesus willingly took upon Himself the punishment that we deserved. On the cross, He who knew no sin became sin for us,[4] bearing the full weight of God's righteous wrath against our rebellion. Jesus didn't just die for your sin; He *became* your sin on the cross. As the prophet Isaiah foretold, "The Lord has laid on Him the iniquity of us all."[5] Jesus endured the punishment that should have been ours.

But the story doesn't end there. Three days later, in a blinding flash of resurrection power, Jesus emerged from the tomb, conquering sin and death once and for all. And now, seated at the

Father's right hand, He offers us a priceless gift: His perfect righteousness.

A miraculous exchange occurs when we place our faith in Christ, turn from our sins, and receive Him as Savior and Lord. Our sin is imputed to Jesus, and His righteousness is imputed to us.

In the words of the apostle Paul, "God made Him who had no sin to be sin for us so that in Him we might become the righteousness of God" (2 Corinthians 5:21). This transaction is so lopsided in our favor, so scandalously generous, that it can only be described as grace in its purest form.

Clothed in Christ

The crucial question is this: Have you accepted this great exchange? Have you cast aside the filthy rags of your own righteousness and received the spotless robe of Christ's perfection?

This is not a matter of mere religious observance or moral striving. It's not about attending church every Sunday or trying your best to be a good person. No, it's about recognizing your utter helplessness before a holy God and accepting His amazing offer of salvation.

When you come to Jesus in repentance and faith, a supernatural transformation takes place. You are clothed in His righteousness,[6] draped in a garment so pure and pristine that it dazzles the eyes of heaven.

From that moment on, when God the Father looks upon you, He no longer sees your sin and failure. Instead, He sees the perfect obedience of His beloved Son. You are accepted, loved, and cherished, not because of anything you have done, but because of everything Christ has done on your behalf.

And here's the glorious truth: You cannot earn or merit this righteousness. It is a gift freely bestowed by a God whose love knows no bounds. All you must do is receive it in humble, grateful submission.

Maybe you think you've gone too far, too stained by sin, to be worthy of such a gift. But hear this: There is no depth of depravity that the blood of Jesus cannot cleanse, no darkness that His light cannot pierce.

Perhaps you're thinking, "This all sounds too good to be true. Surely there's some catch, some hidden price to pay." But I assure you, Christ has already borne the cost on the cross. Your part is to receive, stretch out the empty hands of faith, and accept the richest gift the universe has ever known.

The Urgency of Eternity

I must warn you, the stakes could not be higher. Your eternal destiny hangs in the balance. To reject Christ's offer of righteousness is to court unimaginable tragedy.

Without the covering of His perfection, you will stand exposed and condemned before a holy God. The fleeting pleasures of sin will give way to an eternity of separation and anguish, cut off from the source of all light and love.

I know these are sobering words, but I share them not to condemn but to urge you to make that transaction with Jesus: your sin in trade for His righteousness. Don't let pride or fear hold you back from the most significant decision you will ever make.

Fall on your knees before the King of kings, confess your sin and your need, and receive the robe of His righteousness. It is a garment that will never fade, wear thin, or lose its luster.

And as you rise to your feet, clothed in the radiance of Christ, you will know a joy and a peace that surpasses all understanding. The chains of guilt and shame will fall away, and you will walk in the newness of life, empowered by the very Spirit of God.

This is no mere religious ritual, no empty incantation. It is a profound reality, a seismic shift in the very bedrock of your being. To be clothed in Christ is to be remade from the inside out, to become a new creation, pulsing with the very life of God.

So, once more, I ask you: Will you make the great exchange? Will you trade your sin-stained rags for the spotless robe of Christ's righteousness?

If your answer is yes, then let's bow our heads and seal the transaction right here, right now.

"Jesus Christ, I come before You now, broken and contrite, knowing that my righteousness is as filthy rags. I repent of my sin and rebellion and ask You to forgive me. I believe You died on the cross for my sin and rose again in power and glory.

In humble faith, I now receive the free gift of Your perfect righteousness. I exchange my sin-stained garments for the spotless robe of Your obedience. I trust not in my own works, but in Your finished work on my behalf.

Fill me with Your Holy Spirit and empower me to live a life that glorifies Your name. I am Yours, now and forever. Amen."

If you have prayed this prayer, welcome to the family of God! You are now clothed in the righteousness of Christ, a beloved child of the King.

Wearing the Robe of Righteousness

Perhaps you've been a Christian for some time but still struggle to fully embrace this incredible truth. The old habits of self-reliance and pride can be hard to break. So, let me offer a few practical steps to help you live out your new identity in Christ.

1. Renounce Pride. Pride is the great enemy of grace. It whispers in your ear that you can earn God's favor and are somehow better than others. But the truth is, we are all once helpless sinners in need of a Savior.

So, I invite you to take a profound, symbolic step: Imagine a crown of pride resting upon your head, glittering with self-righteousness. Now, with a decisive motion, reach up and remove that crown. Cast it at the feet of Jesus, declaring, "Lord, I renounce all pride and self-sufficiency. I acknowledge that I am nothing without You."

Feel the weight of pretense and performance lifting from your shoulders. You no longer have to strive to prove your worth. In Christ, you are already accepted, already loved.

2. Picture Yourself Robed In Righteousness. If you are a believer, a follower of Jesus, then you have been irrevocably clothed in His righteousness. This is not a temporary covering but a permanent reality. Your old sin-stained self has been crucified with Christ, and you have been raised to new life in Him.

Take time each day to ponder this glorious truth. When you wake in the morning, picture yourself robed Christ's righteousness, like a king in his royal garments. Throughout the day, whenever feelings of inadequacy or guilt assail you, remember that you are dressed in the very perfection of the Son of God.

Pray prayers like this: "Jesus, thank You for clothing me in Your righteousness. Help me walk in the freedom and joy of knowing You forever accept me. When the enemy whispers lies of condemnation, remind me of the unassailable truth of my new identity."

3. Be Filled With the Spirit. The Christian life is not a matter of gritting our teeth and trying harder. It is a supernatural work of God, empowered by His Holy Spirit. The same Spirit that raised Jesus from the dead now dwells within you, enabling you to live a life that pleases the Father.

So, each morning, invite the Holy Spirit to fill you afresh. Say something like this: "Holy Spirit, I surrender myself to You today. Fill me with Your presence and power. Guide my thoughts, guard my words, and direct my steps. Produce Your fruit in my life: love, joy, peace, patience, kindness, goodness, faithfulness, gentleness, and self-control."

As you learn to walk in step with the Spirit, you will find yourself living out the righteousness of Christ. It will no longer be a matter of striving but of abiding in the Vine, drawing life and strength from Him.

Go Forth in Grace

As this chapter draws to a close, I pray that you will go forth with a new spring in your step and a new song in your heart. You are clothed in the very righteousness of God, a radiant bride, prepared for her heavenly Bridegroom.

You no longer need to labor beneath the weight of guilt and shame. No longer must you strive to earn your way into God's favor. In Christ, you are already accepted, already loved, already righteous.

Walk in the light of this truth. Let it permeate every fiber of your being, transforming how you think, speak, and live. And as you go, share the good news of the great exchange with all who will listen. Point them to the One who traded His crown of glory for a crown of thorns, who bore the penalty of their sin, and who offers them the very righteousness of God.

Now that you're robed in Christ's righteousness, it's time to move on to the next chapter and your next step in breaking up with the enemy and reclaiming peace, hope, and joy.

[1] Matthew 5:48
[2] Isaiah 64:6
[3] Romans 3:23
[4] 2 Corinthians 5:21
[5] Isaiah 53:6
[6] Galatians 3:27

Mike Manuel

Chapter 5

Breaking Up With Unholy Soul Ties

For most of my years as a follower of Jesus, I had never heard the term *soul tie*. It wasn't until I had been a pastor for several years that I not only heard this term but saw how the devil had twisted it to cause emotional pain and suffering for so many people. What God has created for our good, the enemy has perverted to use against us.

As you read on and learn about soul ties, and more importantly, unholy soul ties, it will be eye-opening and maybe initially quite uncomfortable, but ultimately one of the most liberating steps you'll ever take.

What Are Unholy Soul Ties?

As human beings, we are intricately and wonderfully made up of body, soul, and spirit. Our soul—that invisible, eternal part of us encompassing our mind, will, intellect, emotions, and personality—is designed by God to connect and bond with others.

The most sacred of these soul-level connections is between a husband and wife. The Bible tells us that when two people become "one flesh" in marriage, it's not just a physical union but a profound spiritual and emotional oneness.[1] Think soulmate. God's design is to knit our souls with our lifelong partner.

However, the enemy of our souls is constantly seeking to pervert and corrupt God's good gifts. Just as there are holy soul ties, there also exist "unholy soul ties" - spiritual connections forged through sexual activity outside of marriage. When we engage in intimate relations with someone, not our spouse, we inadvertently create a bond that the Bible describes as "becoming one flesh" with that person.[2]

When you establish an unholy soul tie by engaging in sexual behavior that is not biblical, you are disagreeing with God. As you learned in Chapter 2, when you disagree with God, you agree with the enemy; when you agree with the enemy, you give them legal consent to attack you. Consequently, many Christians are being attacked by the enemy through the open door of unholy soul ties.

The Danger of Unholy Soul Ties

Unholy soul ties can impact your life in damaging ways, such as feelings of guilt, shame, and an inability to bond fully with your current or future spouse. I've seen this play out time and time again in the lives of others, both in my pastoral counseling and through stories shared by friends and family members. Spouses may feel like their partner is "holding back" or that something is "missing" in the relationship, and for many, the root cause is unresolved unholy soul ties. Even if the physical relationship ended long ago, those spiritual connections persist.

One of my hobbies is woodworking, and I've learned that gluing two boards together makes one of the strongest joints possible. If, however, you try to peel those two boards apart, they will not come apart cleanly. Each board will have splinters from the other board that are still stuck to it. Soul ties from former relationships are like that: two separate pieces that carry pieces of the other. It's as if a part of that person's soul is still linked to yours, inhibiting your ability to fully bond and connect with your rightful partner. This can breed all sorts of painful emotions - guilt, shame, jealousy, resentment, and an ongoing inability to receive God's healing and restoration.

Satan considers it a victory if he can load you down with guilt and shame while at the same time hamstringing your relationship with your spouse. But his victory is only temporary if you know what to do about it.

Breaking Free From Unholy Soul Ties

The good news is that through the authority Jesus has given you, you can break free from the bondage of unholy soul ties. Just as these ties were formed through sinful sexual activity, they can be severed through repentance and renouncing that connection.

As you work through the steps in the rest of this chapter, you'll begin to experience a new level of intimacy and oneness with your spouse. Fragments of your fragmented and scattered soul will return home, allowing you to build the beautiful, God-ordained marriage you've always dreamed of. If you're single, you will experience the peace that comes from reclaiming the wholeness of your soul from the ravages of the enemy.

If you're reading this and recognizing the negative impact of unholy soul ties in your life, let me assure you - there is hope! God desires to see you set free and your relationships restored to their full potential.

I want to walk you through a practical, biblical process for cutting unholy soul ties and reclaiming your soul's wholeness. You'll learn to identify unholy connections, renounce them, and replace them with healthy, godly relationships.

This journey may not be easy and will require courage and vulnerability. Confronting our past mistakes and how we've allowed the enemy to gain a foothold is never pleasant. But I promise you, the freedom and restoration waiting on the other side is worth it.

Identifying Your Unholy Soul Ties

Now that we've explored the biblical foundations and dangers of unholy soul ties, it's time to walk through the practical process of breaking free from these damaging spiritual connections. This is a crucial next step to experiencing true wholeness and purity in your life and relationships.

The first step in breaking free from unholy soul ties is to get honest and do some personal inventory. Ask the Holy Spirit to reveal to you any relationships or past sexual encounters that have resulted in these damaging spiritual bonds.

Perhaps it's an ex-boyfriend or girlfriend from years ago. It could be a one-night stand you try to keep buried in your memory. Or it could even be an emotional affair or unhealthy attachment to someone at work or church. Unholy soul ties can also be established through pornography and the fantasy life that goes with it. Wherever these unholy ties exist, the Holy Spirit wants to shine His light on them so you can deal with them.

Start by writing down the names of the individuals involved in unholy soul ties. This is an essential exercise because to break free fully, you need to be able to renounce these ties by name. Don't worry; no one will ever see this list.

Don't worry if the list feels long or overwhelming. Remember, the enemy wants to keep you trapped in guilt and shame, but God desires to set you completely free. He can handle the messiness of your past. He specializes in redeeming the most broken and tangled situations.

Renouncing Unholy Soul Ties

Once you've made a list of the unholy soul ties you need to break, it's time to take authority over them in Jesus' name. This step requires humility, courage, and a willingness to be vulnerable before God.

Find a quiet, private space and ask the Holy Spirit to fill you afresh and empower you for this spiritual battle. Then, one by one, begin to renounce those unholy ties, speaking out loud and crossing the names off as you go. Remember, the enemy can't read your mind, so you must verbally break these ties.

Say this aloud for each soul tie on your list: "In the name of Jesus, I renounce the soul tie I formed with _____. I break that connection and declare I belong wholly to my spouse and You alone, Lord. I ask You to sever any lingering spiritual, emotional, or mental attachments and to cleanse and restore my soul."

After declaring this authoritatively and crossing off the names as you go, tear this list into tiny pieces, throw them on the floor, and vigorously stomp on them. As you crush those shredded pieces, declare, "These soul ties are no longer a part of me. They are under my feet, and the enemy has no more legal claim on my life!" You've broken these unholy soul ties; the devil is under your feet!

Don't be surprised if you experience some spiritual resistance or even physical manifestations as you do this. The enemy does not want to relinquish his grip on your life. But take heart - the power of the Holy Spirit is infinitely greater, and Jesus has already won the victory!

Receiving Purity and Freedom

Finally, I want you to anoint yourself with oil as a sign of the Holy Spirit's power to break the yoke of bondage and fill you with purity. Take a small amount of oil (olive oil or a dedicated anointing oil) and place a drop on your forehead as you pray:

"I anoint myself in the name of Jesus and in the power of the Holy Spirit. The yoke of bondage has been broken, and I declare myself free from all unholy soul ties. Lord, fill me with Your purity, wholeness, and peace. Amen"

If pornography has been an issue in your life, now is the time to cancel that legal consent and cast out the spirit of pornography.

These steps are a powerful, tangible way to seal the breaking of those ties and invite the Holy Spirit's restoring work in your life. Receive this anointing with an open heart, knowing that Jesus has set you free.

Replacing Unholy Ties with Healthy Connections

The final step in breaking free from unholy soul ties is replacing those broken, harmful connections with healthy, God-honoring relationships. This is where the real restoration and wholeness begin to take place.

Start by strengthening your bond with your spouse if you are married. Spend intentional time together, be vulnerable with each other, and make your relationship a priority. Invite the Holy Spirit to knit your souls together in a deep, unbreakable way.s

If you're single, ask God to purify your heart and align your desires with His. Seek out godly mentors and peers who can encourage you in purity and help you establish healthy friendships. Be cautious about developing new romantic relationships until you've experienced substantial healing.

Ultimately, the goal is to have your deepest heart connections rooted in your relationship with the Lord. As you draw near to Him, He will fill the empty spaces in your soul that the enemy once tried to occupy. You'll experience wholeness, peace, and joy that overflows into all your other relationships.

One of the enemy's most potent weapons against you is guilt, shame, and condemnation. Hopefully, the steps in this chapter have alleviated some of your guilt and shame. But turn to the next chapter for a complete ridding of all guilt and shame from your life.

---

[1] Ephesians 5:31

[2] 1 Corinthians 6:16

Chapter 6

Breaking Up With Guilt, Shame, and Condemnation

For far too long, too many Christians have allowed guilt, shame, and condemnation to weigh them down, preventing them from fully embracing the abundant life God desires for them. These cunning works of the enemy have trapped people in a cycle of guilt and shame, hindering their ability to accept the Father's unconditional love and grace. If you've been weighed down by guilt, shame, and condemnation, the steps at the end of this chapter will help you break free from these chains and step into the freedom Christ has purchased for you.

The devil is a master at wielding guilt, shame, and condemnation against us. He knows these weapons are incredibly effective in driving a wedge between us and God. When feelings of unworthiness and self-condemnation consume us, our instinct is to hide from the very One who longs to embrace us and heal our wounds.

This pattern is clearly illustrated in the story of Adam and Eve in the Garden of Eden (Genesis 3). Before their disobedience, they enjoyed perfect communion with the Father, walking and talking with Him in the paradise He had lovingly created for them. But everything changed when they gave in to the serpent's temptation and ate the forbidden fruit.

Suddenly, Adam and Eve were acutely aware of their nakedness and vulnerability. When God came walking through the garden, calling out to them, they hid themselves in fear and shame. They had allowed the enemy's lies to distort their perspective, convincing them that they were now exposed and unworthy of God's presence.

The Cycle of Sin and Condemnation

This is the devil's modus operandi. He entices us to sin and then viciously condemns us for it. He lures us into acting against God's will, and then he beats us down with guilt and shame, convincing us that we deserve the condemnation we feel.

Maybe you've fallen into this trap in your own life. Perhaps you made a poor choice or gave in to temptation, and instead of running to God for forgiveness and restoration, you kept your distance from God, convinced that you're too dirty and unworthy for Him to want anything to do with you. You live with a sense of condemnation, allowing it to create distance between you and God.

The Struggle of Believers

You're not alone in this struggle. Countless believers are trapped in this cycle of guilt, shame, and condemnation. They've placed their faith in Jesus for salvation but still wrestle with fully accepting God's unconditional love and grace. We think, "Thank you, Jesus, for saving me and securing my place in heaven. But I'm just too much of a mess for You to truly delight in me."

This muddy veil of guilt, shame, and condemnation hinders our spiritual growth and maturity. It prevents us from fully beholding the glory of the Lord and being transformed into His image.[1] Instead of living in the freedom and joy of our salvation, we remain stuck in a cycle of guilt and shame.

The Church's Role in Perpetuating Guilt and Shame

Tragically, the church has often contributed to this problem, intentionally or unintentionally. Many of us have attended churches where it seemed like the pastor or priest wanted us to have a guilty conscience, as if that would somehow keep us in line. The message we received was we needed to constantly battle against our sinful nature, never genuinely resting in God's grace.

The heavy emphasis on guilt and shame in some churches has driven people away, leaving them feeling like they can't possibly measure up or be accepted by God. They conclude, "I can't go into a church carrying all this guilt and condemnation. I don't want to be a hypocrite like everyone else."

But this is not God's heart. He doesn't want us to live in shame, hiding from Him in fear. Instead, He invites us to draw near confidently, knowing that our sins have been forgiven and we are deeply loved. As we fix our eyes on Him with unveiled faces, we will be transformed from glory to glory by the power of His Spirit.

God's Desire for Our Freedom

God does not want us to live under the oppressive weight of condemnation. The Bible is clear: "There is no condemnation for those in Christ Jesus."[2] The condemnation we feel is not from God; it's a lie from the enemy, designed to keep us from an intimate relationship with our Heavenly Father.

When we surrender our lives to Jesus, He takes our sin, guilt, and shame and nails it to the cross. Colossians 2:14-15 declares that Jesus "canceled the record of the charges against us and took it away by nailing it to the cross. In this way, he disarmed the spiritual rulers and authorities. He shamed them publicly by his victory over them on the cross" (NLT).

Let that truth sink deep into your heart. Jesus has completely erased your sin and the charges the enemy had against you. He triumphed over the powers of darkness, disarming and stripping them of their right to condemn you. The shame, guilt, and condemnation that the devil attempts to heap upon you no longer have any power because Jesus has already dealt with them once and for all at the cross.

Mercy, Grace, and a Clean Conscience

This is God's incredible mercy—not giving us the punishment we deserve for our sins. And it's God's magnificent grace—freely giving us the gift of eternal life despite our unworthiness. Mercy and grace are two sides of the same coin and are the antidote to the poison of guilt, shame, and condemnation.

Satan doesn't want you to understand God's mercy and grace toward you because he wants you to live with a guilty conscience. Why? Because he knows that a guilty conscience keeps you from entering into an intimate relationship with your Father. When your conscience is filled with guilt and shame, the last person you want to be in front of is God. And yet, He strongly desires to have you in His presence.

Hebrews 10:22 shares God's heart as He invites us to "draw near to God with a sincere heart in full assurance of faith, having our hearts sprinkled to cleanse us from a guilty conscience and having our bodies washed with pure water." (NIV). God's desire is not for us to live with the constant burden of a guilty conscience. He has cleansed and purified your heart so that you can come to Him with a clean conscience.

Breaking Up with Guilt, Shame, and Condemnation

It's time to say goodbye to guilt, shame, and condemnation. It's time for you to stop allowing the enemy to use these weapons to keep you from experiencing the fullness of God's love and the freedom Christ purchased for you on the cross. It's time for you to walk in the truth that there is no condemnation for those who belong to Jesus.

In the following section, we'll engage in a practical, symbolic exercise to help wash away the residual effects of guilt, shame, and condemnation. I invite you to join me in this time of ministry as we tangibly remove these burdens and embrace God's mercy and grace.

Breaking Free Through Symbolic Action

Now that we've explored the biblical foundations for breaking up with guilt, shame, and condemnation, it's time to put these principles into practice through a symbolic, prophetic action. These actions will help solidify the Holy Spirit's work in our hearts and minds, empowering us to walk in the freedom Christ has purchased for us.

First, I'd like you to gather a bowl of water. This can be from the tap, a basin, or a cup - the specific container isn't important. What matters is that you have some water available during this time.

Visualizing the Burdens

As you hold your hands over the water, imagine all the guilt, shame, and condemnation you've been carrying. Picture those heavy burdens weighing you down, the lies and accusations the enemy has been using to torment you. These are the tools he's wielded so effectively against you, keeping you trapped in a cycle of self-loathing and separation from God.

Renouncing and Rejecting

Now, I want you to renounce and reject these spiritual forces verbally. Say out loud, "I break up with the spirits of guilt, shame, and condemnation. I divorce you and cast you out in the name of Jesus Christ!" Feel the authority and power behind these words as you reclaim your freedom

Washing Away the Guilt, Shame, and Condemnation

Next, dip your hands into the water and let it flow over your skin. As you do this, declare, "I am washing away all guilt, shame, and condemnation!" Feel the cleansing, refreshing power of the water, and let it symbolize the spiritual cleansing happening within you

Don't be afraid to really get into this. Splash the water on your face, letting it wash away that veil of shame that has kept you from boldly approaching God's throne. Say, "Lord, I come to You with an unveiled face, ready to behold Your glory!"

Receive Healing Prayer

Finally, place your wet hands over your heart and pray for the Lord to heal the wounds and scars caused by years of guilt, shame, and condemnation. Ask Him to touch those deep places, restoring and renewing you supernaturally.

"Lord, I pray for healing to this heart, which has been bruised and scarred by the enemy's attacks. Touch these wounds that no one else can reach, and bring supernatural, immediate, and lasting healing. Remove every trace of the damage caused by guilt, shame, and condemnation. Amen."

Gazing Upon the Father's Face

Once you've prayed this prayer, lift your gaze upward. Look into the face of your Heavenly Father, who sees you as perfect and righteous in Christ. Let His smile fill you, knowing you are deeply loved and accepted. Bask in the glory of the Lord, allowing His transforming power to work in your life.

Repeating the Process

This symbolic action is a powerful tool to help cement the truths we've explored. These physical steps engage our senses and create tangible reminders of the spiritual realities at work. As you obediently participate, you'll find the lingering effects of guilt, shame, and condemnation being washed away.

Be bold and repeat this process as needed. Whenever familiar feelings of unworthiness and condemnation begin to creep back in, return to this ritual. Renew your commitment to breaking up with these weapons of the enemy and affirm your identity as a beloved child of God.

The Journey Ahead

The journey towards freedom may have challenges, but the destination is worth it. As you continue to gaze upon the Lord's face with an unveiled heart, you'll be transformed from glory to glory, becoming more like Him with each passing day. Embrace this new season of intimate relationship and unhindered spiritual growth.

Now that you've been set free from guilt, shame, and condemnation, it will be much easier to accept the Father's life-changing love for you. Turn to the next chapter to learn how to experience more of God's love for you.

A Note from the Author,
Thank you for taking the time to read this book. If you have benefitted from what you've read so far or feel that others would benefit from reading this, please leave a review by using this QR code. Your review helps make this book more visible online so that others can benefit from it as well. Thank you so much for your review! For more resources, visit my website at www.MikeManuel.faith

- Mike

Mike Manuel

---

[1] 2 Corinthians 3:18
[2] Romans 8:1

Chapter 7

Breaking Up With the Orphan Spirit

One of the most significant determining factors in how you live your life comes from how you view God's love for you. At first glance, most people would probably disagree with this premise. It would seem logical that many more significant factors influence our actions, thoughts, and emotions than such a singular concept of love. However, based on biblical truth, my experience as a pastor, and my own experience as a human, I know this to be true. Nothing shapes our lives more than our sense of our Heavenly Father's love for us.

If you have a deep, permeating sense of the Father's unconditional love for you, you will tend to live a more relaxed and peaceful life, knowing you're safe in your Father's care. However, if you live without experiencing that deep, abiding love of the Father, your life will tend to be filled with anxiety, fear, chaos, or a need always to prove yourself. I've lived under both of these scenarios.

You can probably guess which one I recommend. You can also probably guess which one the enemy wants you to live under. The devil and his army of fallen angels work to keep you from experiencing the Father's love in your heart by lying to you about God's intentions toward you. Or, more accurately, the Father's *lack* of intention toward you. They want you to live as a spiritual orphan. In other words, they don't want you to feel safe and secure because you have a loving, caring Father in heaven. No, they want you to live an anxiety-ridden life, wondering what's going to happen to you next because there's no one looking out for you other than yourself.

The orphan spirit is a lying whisper from the enemy that seeks to distort our perception of God and our relationship with Him. It wants us to believe that God is distant, uninvolved, or even disapproving of us. When we live under the influence of the orphan spirit, we feel like spiritual orphans - alone, unprotected, and constantly striving to prove our worth.

This deceptive mindset, perpetuated by the enemy, hinders us from experiencing the depth of God's love and living in the fullness of our identity as His children. In this chapter, we'll explore the characteristics of the orphan spirit, how to break free from its grip, and how to embrace our true identity as sons and daughters who are valued, loved, and cared for by our Father in Heaven.

Characteristics of the Orphan Spirit

Just as many biological orphans have developed specific characteristics and coping mechanisms, spiritual orphans have many of the same issues as they relate to their "orphanhood." Here is a quick overview of some of those characteristics.

1. Anxiety and Fear

One of the hallmark signs of the orphan spirit is a pervasive sense of anxiety and fear, especially about the future. They worry about provision, protection, and whether God will come through for them. This fear often leads to controlling behavior as they attempt to mitigate their anxiety by micromanaging their lives and the lives of others.

2. Identity Crisis and a Search for Significance

The orphan spirit drives people to find their identity and significance in all the wrong places. They may seek validation through their performance, achievements, or the approval of others. They often fall into the trap of comparing themselves to those around them, feeling like they never quite measure up.

3. Mentality of Lack

Those who live as spiritual orphans often operate from a mentality of lack or poverty. They see themselves as the "have-nots," always looking at what others have with envy or resentment. This scarcity mindset closes their eyes to their abundant spiritual blessings in Christ and hinders them from walking in generosity.

4. Relationship Struggles

The orphan spirit can make forming deep, authentic relationships with God and others challenging. They may struggle with trust issues, fearing that if they open up or depend on someone, they'll end up rejected or abandoned. This fear can cause them to keep God and others at arm's length, robbing them of the intimacy and community we were created for.

5. Performance and People-Pleasing

In an attempt to prove their worthiness of love and acceptance, the orphan spirit drives people to perfectionism and people-pleasing. They exhaust themselves trying to earn God's approval and the approval of others through their performance. They fear rejection, so they mold themselves to fit others' expectations, often at the expense of their well-being and authenticity.

6. Distorted View of Authority

For those operating under an orphan spirit, authority figures - including God - can be viewed as sources of pain or punishment rather than protection and provision. This is often rooted in experiences of abuse, neglect, or inconsistency from parental figures. As a result, they may struggle to trust God's heart for them, seeing Him as a harsh taskmaster rather than a loving Father.

These characteristics in the lives of spiritual orphans don't form on their own; they're cultivated and nourished by the enemy in the souls of unsuspecting victims. And it all starts by getting people to question God's love for them.

The Uniqueness of Being God's Child

Contrary to popular belief, not everyone is a child of God. John 1:12 says, "But to all who believed him and accepted him, he gave the right to become children of God." (NLT) God is God to everyone, but He's Father only to the believer. God indeed loves everyone, but there's something special about a father's love for his own children.

In addition to being born into God's family through the rebirth that comes through faith in Jesus, the Bible also says God adopts us.

In Galatians 4:4-7, Paul writes, "But when the right time came, God sent his Son, born of a woman, subject to the law. God sent him to buy freedom for us, who were slaves to the law so that he could adopt us as his very own children. And because we are his children, God has sent the Spirit of his Son into our hearts, prompting us to call out, 'Abba, Father.' Now you are no longer a slave but God's own child. And since you are his child, God has made you his heir." (NIV)

If we're born into God's family by being born again when we believed, why do we need to be adopted?

Here's the reason: Our spiritual adoption is a powerful truth that dismantles the lies of the orphan spirit. In biblical culture, adoption was a significant legal process that granted the adopted child full rights and privileges within the family, including inheritance rights. When God adopts us, He gives us full standing as His children, with all the benefits and blessings that come with being part of His family.

You can now see why Satan wants to keep believers from fully understanding the benefits of being a born-again adopted child of God.

Receiving a Revelation of the Father's Love

While we may intellectually know that God loves us, the orphan spirit hinders us from fully receiving and experiencing that love in our hearts. This is where the ministry of the Holy Spirit comes in. Romans 8:15-16 tells us, "So you have not received a spirit that makes you fearful slaves. Instead, you received God's Spirit when he adopted you as his own children. Now we call him, 'Abba, Father.' For his Spirit joins with our spirit to affirm that we are God's children." (NIV)

The Holy Spirit's role is to pour God's love into our hearts and give us a deep, abiding revelation of our identity as beloved children of God.[1] This revelation goes beyond head knowledge; it is a truth that permeates our entire being, healing the wounds inflicted by the orphan spirit and enabling us to live from a place of security and belongingness.

When we cry out "Abba, Father," it is a term of endearment, similar to "Daddy" or "Papa." It speaks of intimacy, trust, and the assurance that we are cherished and cared for by our heavenly Father. As we learn to approach God with this kind of childlike faith and dependence, the grip of the orphan spirit begins to loosen.

Breaking Free from the Orphan Spirit

In this time of ministry, I'm going to guide you through the process of casting out the orphan spirit and receiving a fresh revelation of the Father's love. Are you ready to be free?

First, I want you to take a moment and get some anointing oil. Place a small dab on your finger. As you do this, I want you to focus on the fact that you are about to take authority over the orphan spirit plaguing you.

Now, as you hold that oil, I want you to anoint yourself and declare out loud, "In the name of Jesus, I cast out the orphan spirit. You have no place in my life anymore!"

Put some conviction behind those words. Make sure you're commanding that orphan spirit to leave. Tell it, "I divorce you, I break up with you. Take all your anxiety, your fear, your attachment issues, your trust problems, and your rejection - take it all and go, in Jesus' name!"

The enemy has no authority over you. You are a child of the King, and the orphan spirit has to submit to Jesus' name. So declare it boldly—the orphan spirit is gone!

Receiving the Father's Love

Now that you have taken authority over that spirit, it's time to fill the void that it has left. The enemy always tries to steal, kill, and destroy, but Jesus came to give us life in abundance.

So put your hand over your heart and get ready to receive. Pray this prayer and believe the

Holy Spirit will pour the Father's extravagant love into your heart in a fresh, powerful way.

"Holy Spirit, in the name of Jesus, I ask that you would fill me to overflowing with the revelation of the Father's love. Show me how proud He is of me. Please remind me how special and cherished I am as your beloved child.

Holy Spirit, I invite you to minister the Father's love to me in a tangible way. Flood my heart, mind, and soul with the truth of my identity as your dearly loved son/daughter. Let me feel it, not just know it in my head.

Thank You, Father, for your tremendous love for me. I receive it now, in Jesus' name. Amen"

Receive it. Receive the Father's affection, delight, and unconditional acceptance. Let it wash over you and transform you from the inside out. This love is life-changing—it's what will set you fully free from the orphan spirit for good.

Just take a moment and bask in the Father's love. Allow it to sink deep within you, penetrating your "knower." This is your true reality - you are God's cherished child, and nothing can change that.

So let the love of the Father fill you now. Let it restore, renew, and revive every area the orphan spirit has touched. You are home. You are loved. You are free.

---

[1] Romans 5:5

Mike Manuel

Chapter 8

Breaking Up With Unforgiveness

Unforgiveness is that simmering resentment we carry toward those who have wronged us, the hurt that we replay over and over in our minds, the bitterness we nurse in our hearts. It can feel justified, even righteous, at times. But the truth is, unforgiveness is a trap that ensnares us, opens a door to the enemy, and blocks the full flow of God's power in our lives.

The Unforgiving Servant

Jesus addressed this in Matthew 18 with the story of the unforgiving servant. The king had forgiven this man an enormous debt - ten thousand talents, equivalent to millions in today's money. Unfathomable forgiveness! Yet when a fellow servant owed him a mere hundred denarii (a tiny fraction of what he'd been forgiven), he refused to extend mercy. Instead, he had the man thrown in prison until he could pay the debt.

When word got back to the king, he was furious. He called the servant in and said, "You wicked servant! I forgave you all that debt because you pleaded with me. Shouldn't you have had mercy on your fellow servant just as I had on you?" In anger, the king turned the unforgiving servant over to the jailers to be tortured until he paid back all he owed.

Alignment with the Enemy

Ouch. Torture? Jailers? Surely, this is just a metaphor, right? A vivid word picture to make a point about God's expectations regarding forgiveness? Well, yes and no. You see, God is not a jailer or a torturer. He is a good Father, abounding in mercy. But there is a very real enemy of our souls - Satan and his demonic realm. They are the torturers and the jailers. And when we withhold forgiveness, we unwittingly align ourselves with them and open the door for torment in our lives.

The Poison of Unforgiveness

In over two decades of pastoral ministry, I've seen this repeatedly: believers who are stuck, stagnant, and plagued with defeat and oppression.

As I've probed deeper, unforgiveness is almost always a key factor: a spouse's betrayal, a friend's cruel words, or a parent's abuse or neglect. The wounds are real, and the pain is raw. But harboring unforgiveness is like drinking poison and expecting the other person to die. It destroys us from the inside out.

Why Forgiveness is Hard

So why is it so hard to forgive? For one, we often equate forgiveness with condoning what was done to us. We think that by forgiving, we're saying it was okay or excusable. But that's not what forgiveness is at all. The offense was real. The mistreatment was wrong. Forgiveness doesn't whitewash that. It simply releases the person from the debt they owe us.

Another reason we resist forgiveness is because we confuse it with forgetting. "I'll never forget what they did to me!" we declare. And in a sense, that's probably true. Forgiveness doesn't erase the memory. But it does drain the memory of its power to control us. It's like pulling the teeth of a venomous snake. The snake is still in your memory, but its ability to keep poisoning you is gone.

Forgiveness is a Faith Issue

Ultimately, unforgiveness is hard because it's a faith issue. It requires fully entrusting the person and situation to God. We're afraid that if we release them, they'll get away with it. We fear God won't deal with them as severely as we want Him to. After all, He's big on mercy and redemption—but not us. We prefer retaliation and retribution.

But here's the pivotal question - do you trust God enough to release that person to Him? To relinquish your right to get even and let God handle it His way, in His timing? It's an act of faith to open your clenched fist and say, "God, this person is Yours to deal with now. I trust You with this."

The Bait of Offense

Jesus framed unforgiveness in Luke 17 by saying offenses will come - it's inevitable in a broken world. But He described those offenses as a "trap." The Greek word used there is *scandalon*, which refers to the trigger in a trap, the part that holds the bait. You see, an offense is bait. It's tempting to grab hold of it and camp there, nursing our wound. But it's a setup! The enemy knows if he can lure us into unforgiveness, he's got us trapped.

It reminds me of a nature documentary I once saw about hunting monkeys for food in certain parts of the world. The hunters take a small cage with bars just wide enough for the monkey to stick its hand through. They place the monkey's favorite fruit inside, tether the cage to the ground, and wait along the trail. The monkey comes along, smells the fruit, and reaches in to grab it. But it can't pull it back out once its hand is clasped around that fruit.

Meanwhile, the hunters approach with clubs, ready to beat them over the head. The monkey sees them coming yet won't release the fruit to save its life. It's trapped by the bait, caught by its refusal to let go.

That's exactly the predicament we find ourselves in when we hold on to unforgiveness. The enemy comes with his clubs of torment, oppression, and bondage, and the whole time, we could release ourselves simply by letting go of the offense! But we make the same foolish choice as that monkey, clinging to the bait that traps us. We think we're punishing the one who hurt us, but we're only hurting ourselves.

The Real-World Power of Forgiveness

I saw this illustrated vividly with a woman I was counseling years ago. She had suffered terrible mistreatment from her mother growing up - constant criticism, physical abuse, and shaming. The wounds were deep, and the unforgiveness was choking the life out of her. As we talked and prayed, she realized the only way to freedom was to release her mother and the years of hurt. With tears streaming, she opened her fists and let it go, forgiving her mother and repenting for holding onto bitterness for so long.

What happened next was remarkable. This woman, who had suffered knee pain for years, suddenly fell to the floor laughing and weeping. I thought at first it was just emotion and relief. But then I realized - she was crawling around on her hands and knees! She looked up at me, crying and giggling, and said, "They don't hurt! For the first time in years, my knees don't hurt!" Unforgiveness had been a door for chronic pain in her body. As she released it, healing flowed.

That wasn't the first or last time I observed physical healing through forgiveness. That's the power of forgiveness. It closes the door to the enemy's harassment and opens the gates for God's healing power to flow.

Uprooting the Bitter Root

But there's a critical second step - uprooting bitterness. Hebrews 12:15 warns about a "bitter root" growing up to cause trouble and defile us. The passage urges us not to fall short of God's grace by allowing bitterness to spring up. The original language indicates that bitterness causes us to "lag behind" in our spiritual progress. It stunts our spiritual growth!

If you've ever battled a stubborn weed in your garden, you know that just cutting off the top doesn't solve the problem. As long as that root remains, the weed will come right back. Bitterness is like that. We can go through the motions of forgiving, but if we don't dig out the root, it will continue to inject its poison into our lives, choking out the good things God wants to grow in us.

We uproot bitterness in the same way we deal with unforgiveness: by releasing it to God. We acknowledge the bitterness, repent, and act it out by physically pulling up the roots. When I'm praying for people through this, I often have them make a symbolic physical action of ripping out the bitter root and throwing it away. It may feel silly, but engaging our bodies in prophetic declarations is powerful!

Breaking Up with Unforgiveness

Now that we've explored the trap of unforgiveness and the freedom that comes from releasing it, let's walk through some practical steps to apply in your own life. Remember, forgiveness is not a feeling; it's a choice. It's an act of your will to release the person and the offense to God. You may not feel like forgiving, but as you choose to trust God in this area, your feelings will transform from bitterness, anger, and resentment to peace and contentment. You may even experience physical healing!

Step 1: Identify Who You Need to Forgive

Take a few moments now and ask the Holy Spirit to reveal anyone you're holding unforgiveness towards. Take your time with this process. Allow God to bring faces and names to mind. It may be a parent who neglected you, a spouse who betrayed you, or a friend who rejected you. As names and faces come to mind, jot them down so you remember them.

For some of you, an incident from long ago that you thought was resolved may surface. That's okay. If it's coming to mind now, there's likely some residue of unforgiveness there that needs to be dealt with. Just add it to your list.

If you're having trouble identifying anyone, here are some prompts that may help:

- Who has hurt me deeply?

- Who am I avoiding or secretly hoping never to run into?

- Who do I often rehearse arguments with in my mind?

- Who do I feel owes me an apology?

- Is there anyone I secretly hope will fail or get what they deserve?

Remember, forgiveness isn't saying what they did was okay. It's saying you're releasing your right to get even and trusting God to deal with it justly. It's getting yourself out of the middle.

Step 2: Verbally Release Each Person

Now, I want you to pause after each name on your list and verbally release that person to God. This is important because while God looks at your heart, the enemy can only hear what's verbalized. By speaking out your forgiveness, you're serving notice to the spiritual realm that you're closing the door of unforgiveness the enemy has been using to torment you. It's how you cancel their legal consent.

Here's an example of how you can phrase it:

"In the name of Jesus, I forgive (name). I release them and the debt they owe me. They no longer owe me anything. I place them in Your hands, God, and trust You to deal with them justly. I am free from this offense, and they are free from my judgment."

Go through each person on your list and verbally release them like this. Take your time. This is not a race. Keep going until every person on your list has been released through verbal forgiveness. Some names may elicit strong emotions. That's okay. Let the tears flow if needed. Revisiting past hurts can be very difficult. But it's part of the forgiveness process.

Step 3: Forgive Yourself

One of the people you may need to forgive is yourself. So often, we carry guilt, shame, and self-blame for things in our past. But Romans 8:1 says there is no condemnation for those in Christ Jesus. If God has forgiven you, who are you to withhold forgiveness from yourself?

If you're struggling to forgive yourself, pray this aloud:

"Father God, I confess I've been holding unforgiveness towards myself for (list specifics). I receive Your total forgiveness for my sins through the blood of Jesus. I choose now to extend that same forgiveness to myself. I release myself from all guilt, shame, and self-condemnation. I declare I am a new creation in Christ. The old is gone; the new has come! In Jesus' name, amen."

Step 4: Uproot Any Bitterness

As you've released these people who have hurt you, ask the Holy Spirit if any roots of bitterness have grown up in your heart towards them. Remember, bitterness is not incompatible with forgiveness. You can forgive someone and still harbor bitterness. That's why this is a separate step.

If you sense any bitterness, let's do a prophetic act to uproot it now. Physically pretend to grab that bitter root and yank it out of the ground of your inner person. As you do, pray this:

"Holy Spirit, I repent for allowing a root of bitterness to grow up in my heart towards (name). I renounce this bitterness now. It has no place in me. I command it to be uprooted and cast out in Jesus' name. I declare my heart is good soil for the fruit of the Spirit to grow. Fill me now with Your love, joy, peace, patience, kindness, goodness, faithfulness, gentleness, and self-control. In Jesus' name, amen."

Step 5: Bless Those Who Hurt You

This last step may be very difficult, but it's very healing. In Luke 6:28, Jesus tells us to "bless those who curse you, pray for those who mistreat you." It's contrary to our flesh to bless someone who has hurt us, but in doing so, we cut off any remnant of unforgiveness and release a divine transaction.

Pray this over each person as you feel led:

"Father, I ask You to bless (name). Pour out Your goodness and mercy over their life. Reveal Your love and kindness to them. Draw them close to Your heart. Heal their wounds and set them free. Cause everything the enemy meant for evil to be turned for good in their life. May they come to know You intimately. In Jesus' name, amen."

Walking in Freedom

As you walk out these steps, expect to feel a heaviness lift off your life. Expect a new level of intimacy with God and a fresh sensitivity to the Holy Spirit. When we align our hearts with His heart through forgiveness, it opens a portal for His unhindered power and blessing to flow.

If any of these people you've forgiven are still in your life, it doesn't mean you have to trust them or be best friends. Forgiveness and trust are two separate things. Trust must be earned over time. But you can rest, knowing you've done your part to close the door to the enemy and walk in the freedom and blessing Jesus purchased for you.

Remember, forgiveness is not a one-time event. As you continue walking with Christ, He'll likely bring up other layers that must be worked through. That's okay. It's evidence of His love and desire to make you whole.

This is how we break up with unforgiveness - through releasing and uprooting. It's a choice to trust God with the people and pain of our past. As we do, expect a fresh flow of God's grace! Expect accelerated growth and healing. Expect relationships to mend and favor to be unleashed. God's forgiveness towards you is complete. Now, freely give what you have freely received. Blessings await on the other side of release!

Chapter 9

Breaking Up With Self-Pity

Pity, in and of itself, is not a bad thing. It is a natural human emotion that allows us to empathize with others who are going through difficult times. When we experience loss, disappointment, or misfortune, it is appropriate to feel sorrow and grief. The Bible even encourages us to pity others who are suffering.[1] However, there is a significant difference between healthy pity and the destructive force of self-pity.

Self-pity is like pity on steroids. It causes us to become excessively focused on our misfortunes, losses, and disappointments to an unhealthy degree. When we allow ourselves to wallow in self-pity, we open the door for the enemy to speak lies into our minds and steal our hope.

The Enemy's Tactics: Stealing Our Hope

The enemy is cunning in his approach to leading you into self-pity. He begins by agreeing with you that your situation is indeed terrible. He whispers thoughts like, "This is really bad. It's probably not going to get better. Your world has changed forever." His goal is to steal your hope and make you believe that your current circumstances will never improve.

The Bible warns us in Proverbs 13:12, "Hope deferred makes the heart sick." (NIV) When we lose hope for the future, our hearts become overwhelmed with despair and hopelessness. This is precisely where the enemy wants us to stay – trapped in a cycle of self-pity and hopelessness.

The enemy tries to convince us that our current struggles are the "new normal" and that things will never improve. He wants us to give up any expectation of God's power working in our lives and our future. But we must remember what God's Word promises us in Jeremiah 29:11, "For I know the plans I have for you, declares the Lord, plans to prosper you and not to harm you, plans to give you hope and a future." (NIV) We must cling to this promise and not allow the enemy to steal our hope.

The Lie of "My Cross to Bear"

As the enemy continues his attack, he shifts his tactics to seemingly sympathize with us in our struggles. He whispers thoughts like, "You're so strong. No one understands what you're going through. I guess this is just your cross to bear." We may start to believe the lie that our suffering is some sort of holy burden that we alone must carry.

However, this is a dangerous misconception. When the Bible talks about "taking up our cross," it's referring to the act of crucifying our old sinful nature and following Christ.[2] It's not about bearing the weight of misfortune or suffering alone. Jesus Himself said in Matthew 11:30, "For my yoke is easy and my burden is light." (NIV). He invites us to give our burdens and struggles to Him, not to carry them on our own.

The Addiction of Condolences

As we continue to wallow in self-pity, the enemy begins to dole out condolences that stroke our ego. He whispers thoughts like, "You are so amazing for enduring this. I don't know how you do it. You are so strong!" Even well-meaning friends and loved ones may echo these sentiments, trying to encourage us in our struggles.

While their encouragement comes from a place of love and concern, the enemy can twist these condolences to make us feel a false sense of heroism and significance in our suffering. We may even begin to crave the attention and validation that comes with being seen as "strong" in the face of adversity.

However, this is a dangerous trap. We can become addicted to the constant condolences and attention, finding our worth and identity in our struggles rather than in Christ. We must remember that we are not the heroes of our own story – Jesus Christ is the true hero who carried our burdens to the cross.

Giving Our Burdens to Jesus

The truth is, we were never meant to carry the weight of our burdens and struggles alone. Jesus Christ already bore the ultimate burden when He died on the cross. He invites us to cast all our cares and anxieties on Him because He cares for us.[3]

When we find ourselves trapped in the cycle of self-pity, we must consciously choose to give our burdens to Christ. This doesn't mean that our struggles will magically disappear, but it does mean that we don't have to face them alone. We can trust that God is with us and has a plan and purpose for our lives, even amid difficult circumstances.

Clinging to God's Promises

To break free from the trap of self-pity, we must replace the enemy's lies with the truth of God's Word. Proverbs 23:18 promises us, "There is surely a future hope for you, and your hope will not be cut off" (NIV). No matter what the enemy tries to tell us, we have a secure hope and future in Christ.

We must agree with God's promises rather than the enemy's lies. God's Word is full of promises that we can cling to in times of struggle and despair. Here are just a few:

"The Lord is close to the brokenhearted and saves those who are crushed in spirit." (Psalm 34:18 NIV)

"He heals the brokenhearted and binds up their wounds." (Psalm 147:3 NIV)

"Weeping may endure for a night, but joy comes in the morning." (Psalm 30:5 NKJV)

"And we know that in all things God works for the good of those who love him, who have been called according to his purpose." (Romans 8:28 NIV)

When we meditate on these promises and choose to believe them over the lies of the enemy, we find hope and strength to persevere through even the darkest times.

Living in Hope and Victory

Breaking up with self-pity is not a one-time event but a daily choice to live in the hope and victory that Christ has secured for us. It requires us to be vigilant in guarding our thoughts and believing God's truth over the enemy's lies.

But the good news is that we don't have to do it alone. Christ is with us every step of the way, offering us His strength, comfort, and grace. When we give our burdens to Him and choose to trust in His promises, we can face even the darkest times with hope and confidence.

As we break free from the trap of self-pity and learn to live in God's hope and provision, we will begin to see His power at work in our lives in new and exciting ways. We will experience joy and peace knowing that our hope and future are secure in Him.

I encourage you to make the choice today to break up with self-pity and embrace the abundant life that Jesus came to give us. Let us fix our eyes on Him, the author and perfecter of our faith, and run with perseverance the race marked out for us.[4] For in Christ, we have hope and a glorious future that cannot be taken away from us.

Breaking Up with Self-Pity

Breaking up with self-pity is not easy, but it's a necessary step to live in the freedom and victory that Jesus died to give you. It requires a daily choice to give your burdens and struggles to Him, to cling to His promises, and to reject the enemy's lies.

As you take these steps and choose to break up with self-pity, you will begin to experience the freedom and joy that comes from living in the hope and victory of Jesus.

Next, we will dive into a practical self-ministry segment that will guide you through the process of repentance, renouncing self-pity, and receiving the hope and expectation that can only be found in God.

Step 1: Repentance - Making Jesus the Hero

Remember, repentance is a conversation with Jesus, not the enemy. Be respectful and reverent as you approach the throne of grace.

The first step in breaking up with self-pity is to recognize that we have often made ourselves the hero of our own story, rather than giving that rightful place to Jesus. We need to repent, which means turning away from our self-centered perspective and toward Jesus.

Pray this prayer of repentance, or use your own words:

"Jesus, please forgive me for being the hero. I'm not the hero. You're the hero. Thank you for forgiving me. I proclaim you now as my hero. Amen"

Step 2: Anointing and Renouncing Self-Pity

Now that you have repented and acknowledged Jesus as the true hero, it's time to take authority over the spirit of self-pity and cast it out of your life. This powerful symbolic act demonstrates your faith and your determination to break free from self-pity's influence.

Take some anointing oil and apply it to yourself as a sign of consecration and dedication to God and as a declaration of breaking the yoke of bondage. As you do this, speak this to the enemy:

"In the name of Jesus, I tell the spirit of self-pity to leave. I cast out the spirit of self-pity. Self-pity, I break all ties with you now in Jesus' name. I cancel your legal consent, your legal agreement, and I cast you out now, in Jesus' name."

By anointing yourself and renouncing self-pity, you declare that you no longer agree with its lies and deception. You are breaking the power of hopelessness and lack of expectation.

Step 3: Receiving Hope and Expectation

Having repented and renounced self-pity, you are now ready to receive hope and a sense of expectation. Open your hands in a posture of receptivity, and allow the Holy Spirit to minister to you.

As you pray this prayer, believe that God is faithful to His promises. He is pouring hope and expectation into your life, replacing the hopelessness and despair that self-pity has brought. Receive this impartation by faith, knowing God has great things in store for you.

Pray this prayer:

"Holy Spirit, in the name of Jesus, I ask you to fill me with hope and expectation. I ask you now to fill me with hope in that place where hopelessness resided. Fill my soul with hope, my heart with hope, and my mind with hope. You promised in your Word, God, that hope would not be cut off. You have not cut off my hope. Fill me now with hope and expectation. Let me know that you *are* moving on my behalf and *will* move on my behalf. I can expect you to do great things in my life. Restore my hope, and give me more hope than I've ever had. Pour that hope into me now, in Jesus' name. Amen."

Breaking up with self-pity is a process, but by following these steps of repentance, renunciation, and receiving hope, you are well on your way to experiencing the freedom and joy that God has for you. Remember, Jesus is the hero of your story, and He has a promising future planned for you. Trust in His love and faithfulness, and watch as

He transforms your life with His hope and expectation.

---

[1] Romans 12:15

[2] Luke 9:23

[3] 1 Peter 5:7

[4] Hebrews 12:1-2

Mike Manuel

Chapter 10

Breaking Up With The Religious Spirit

In a shrewd, sleight-of-hand move, Satan has infiltrated the Church with the goal of keeping people from entering into an intimate relationship with God and walking in the fruit of the Spirit. What's even more despicable is that he uses churchgoers to carry out this work. Ironically, most people who attend church are unaware of this tactic of the enemy, while most non-churched people can smell this from a mile away. They don't know what they're smelling; they only know that they don't like it.

While the enemy has used this tactic for thousands of years, it has only recently been named the *religious spirit*.

Ruining Religion

Many of you have probably connected the word *religious* always to mean something good. And there certainly are times when the words *religion* or *religious* can be used in a good connotation. However, most of the time, when Jesus referred to religious activity, it wasn't connected to anything good. The Pharisees were very religious but missed the whole point about being godly. Even now, in our time, religious activity can often become a deceptive substitute for living as a true follower of Jesus.

The religious spirit is a tactic of Satan to fill the Church with religious rituals and legalism while at the same time emptying it of true godliness and God's supernatural power.

Satan is crafty. He knows he can't hinder God's work by appearing overtly evil. He achieves far more by subtly misdirecting people's understanding of God's desires - His will and ways. By making religiosity look godly and appealing, he leads earnest but misguided people away from an authentic relationship with God. God's character, will, and ways are misrepresented when the religious spirit is at work.

The Form Without the Power

The religious spirit entices people to establish a man-made religious system and call it obedience to God. It fulfills 2 Timothy 3:5, "having a form of godliness but denying its power." People under the influence of the religious spirit have the Christian "look" down pat but lack the vibrant spiritual life that can only come through intimacy with Jesus.

True humility is replaced by false humility in this deceptive economy—being proud of one's religiosity. People with a religious spirit are some of the most prideful people you'll meet, yet in their minds, they're some of the most humble people they know.

A person with a religious spirit craves human power and approval more than God's power and presence. They're more focused on building their own kingdom rather than God's kingdom. They show lots of religious activity but exhibit very little of the Holy Spirit's fruit and are more concerned with propping up their religious reputation than passionately pursuing Jesus.

Telltale Signs of the Religious Spirit

How can you discern if you're operating under the influence of the religious spirit? Here are some key characteristics:

1. Appearance-Driven Faith

People with a religious spirit are preoccupied with things like what people wear to church, as if that were a measure of spirituality. They judge and alienate others because they don't fit their religious mold. God looks at the heart, not the external trappings.[1]

2. Performance-based Christianity

People with a religious spirit have a performance-driven view of Christianity, striving to earn God's love and favor through religious activity. Outwardly, they preach grace, but inwardly, they live under the crushing weight of legalism. Often, they're worn out from trying to be "good enough," not acknowledging that God's love for them is based on Christ's performance, not theirs. They don't rest in His finished work.

3. Behavior Modification Instead of Heart Transformation

People with a religious spirit focus all their energy on conforming their outward behavior (and that of others) to religious standards. They ignore the deeper work God wants to do in their heart. Jesus reserved His harshest words for religious hypocrites who cleaned the outside of the cup while neglecting the inside.[2]

4. Critic Instead of Encourager

People with a religious spirit are so preoccupied with scrutinizing others' relationships with God that they fail to look in the mirror. They hold everyone else to the same impossible standard of perfection that they hold themselves to. In the process, they miss opportunities to love, encourage, and build up their brothers and sisters. If you find yourself constantly criticizing others' faith, it indicates that you're under the influence of a religious spirit.

5. Dutiful Service Instead of Passionate Devotion

For those influenced by the religious spirit, Christian service is fueled by duty and obligation rather than love for God. Ministry is a joyless burden, not an outpouring of a relationship with Jesus. They think they're serving Jesus, but they're really serving religion.

6. Misplaced Identity

The core identity of someone under the influence of the religious spirit is wholly enmeshed in what they do for God and how they are perceived at church. They have no idea who they are apart from their religious persona and performance. They need the approval of others to feel significant instead of having their identity firmly anchored in Christ's unshakeable love for them.

7. Controlling Instead of Serving

Many people with a religious spirit wield their spiritual authority like a hammer, seeking to control and conform people rather than humbly serving them. Their leadership style resembles the heavy-handed style of the Pharisees rather than the foot-washing servanthood of Jesus. Church leaders with a religious spirit are more concerned with their power and agenda than empowering others to walk with God.

Breaking Free from the Religious Spirit

If you recognize the fingerprints of the religious spirit in your life, please don't despair. Freedom is available in Christ! Here are some steps that will guide you through the process of repentance, renouncing, and breaking free from the religious spirit.

Step 1. Repent

Pray this prayer of repentance, or use your own words:

"Jesus, please forgive me for any participation with the religious spirit. I repent of my religious pride and my self-righteousness. I repent of misrepresenting You in any way, and I now humbly surrender my "Good Christian" mask to You. I ask that I not only know Your truth, but also Your heart. Thank you for forgiving me. Amen"

Step 2. Anointing and Renouncing the Religious Spirit

Now that you have repented from participating with the religious spirit, it's time to take authority over it and cast it out of your life. This powerful symbolic act demonstrates your faith and determination to break free from the religious spirit's influence.

Take some anointing oil and apply it to yourself as a sign of consecration and dedication to God and as a declaration of breaking the yoke of bondage. As you do this, speak this boldly to the enemy:

"In the name of Jesus, I tell the religious spirit to leave. I cast you out now, in Jesus' name. I cancel any legal consent I have given you, and I break all ties with you now in the name of Jesus."

By anointing yourself and renouncing the religious spirit, you declare that you no longer agree with its lies and deception. You are breaking the power of empty religious activity in your life.

3. Rekindle Your First Love

Make a conscious choice to prioritize pursuing intimacy with Jesus over maintaining a religious reputation. Carve out unhurried time in God's presence, and you will experience more love and passion for Him. Learn to hear His voice and experience His heart in fresh ways. Make intimacy with Jesus the non-negotiable center of your life, not an afterthought tacked onto your religious duties.

Embracing Authentic Christianity

Nothing is more fulfilling or powerful than knowing Jesus personally and learning to walk in step with His Spirit. Religion is a cheap, burdensome substitute that will always leave you empty. Jesus didn't die on the cross to make you religious—He died to set you free to enjoy an intimate, passionate relationship with Him.

I encourage you to embrace the authentic, world-changing faith modeled in the Book of Acts and made possible by the cross. Fix your eyes on Jesus, the Author and Perfecter of your faith. As you abide in Him and He abides in you, you will bear much fruit for God's Kingdom and experience the abundant life Jesus promised you. This is what you were made for!

---

[1] 1 Samuel 16:7

[2] Matthew 23:25-26

Mike Manuel

Chapter 11

Closing Commonly-Opened Doors

Throughout this book, we've been learning how Christians can find themselves struggling against spiritual oppression, persistent sins, and negative emotions, unaware that they have opened doorways in their lives that grant the enemy access and influence. These "open doors" often arise subtly through areas where we have unknowingly agreed with the enemy's lies or come into disagreement with God's truth. To experience the fullness of freedom Jesus purchased for us, we must learn to identify these open doors, renounce our agreement with the enemy, and wholeheartedly embrace God's perspective instead.

In my own journey, I've discovered that recognizing and closing these doors is not a one-time event but an ongoing process in our spiritual growth. Early in my walk with God, I encountered many typical entry points the enemy exploits, such as unconfessed sin, harboring unforgiveness, and believing lies spoken over me. Each time I renounced my agreement with the enemy and aligned myself with God's word, I experienced greater freedom and wholeness.

One of the main points of this book is that we cannot simply tell the enemy to leave; we must first revoke any permission we've granted him. Just as a landlord must cancel a tenant's lease before evicting them, we need to annul any legal right the enemy claims in our lives through open doors. This involves recognizing specific ways we've agreed with the enemy, renouncing them, and repenting before God for any agreement we've made with darkness.

Through years of ministering deliverance to others and examining Scripture, I've identified several doorways the enemy frequently leverages to gain influence in our lives. As you read through these brief descriptions, ask the Holy Spirit to reveal any doors you may have opened to the enemy through these words or actions. After each description, there's a simple script for you to close that door by renouncing your involvement with the enemy. As you learned earlier, be sure to speak this verbally. Following the renunciation is a simple prayer of repentance to the Lord.

1. Unsubmitted Sin

When we knowingly persist in sin, rationalizing or excusing it, we create an open door for the enemy. While all believers struggle with sin, unrepentant, continued sin is the same as saying to God, "I know this displeases You, but I'm going to keep doing it anyway." This intentional disobedience grants the enemy legal access to your soul. The remedy is sincere confession and repentance, bringing our struggles into the light and receiving God's forgiveness.[1]

Renounce: "Demons and evil spirits, I close all doors I have opened through un-submitted sin. I break all agreements with you."

Repent: "Jesus, I submit these sins to you now. I confess they are wrong, and I accept your forgiveness. Thank you for forgiving me."

2. Occult Involvement

Engaging with any practice that accesses spiritual power apart from the Holy Spirit opens significant doors for the enemy. This includes consulting psychics, using Ouija boards, tarot cards, participating in séances, fortune-telling, channeling, and many New Age practices. While some dabble in these activities out of curiosity, God forbids them because they are genuine gateways for demonic footholds.[2] Renounce all occult participation and close those doors.

Renounce: "Demons and evil spirits, I renounce any involvement with the occult. I break all agreements that I, or my ancestors before me, made with you. Your hold over me and my family ends now."

Repent: "Jesus, please forgive me and my family for any involvement, known or unknown, with the occult. I repent in Jesus' name. Thank you for forgiving me."

3. Hypnosis

When we allow another person or process to bypass our conscious mind and embed suggestions in our subconscious, we relinquish control in a way God never intended. Hypnosis, whether for entertainment or behavior modification, opens us up to enemy influence because we've allowed someone else to program us. If you've participated in hypnosis, break your agreement with this practice.

Renounce: "Demons and evil spirits, I renounce my agreement to be hypnotized. I break all agreements that I made with you while under hypnosis."

Repent: "Jesus, please forgive me for surrendering my soul to hypnosis. I repent in Jesus' name. Thank you for forgiving me."

4. Secret Societies

Joining organizations like the Freemasons or other groups that require secret oaths, vows, and secret rituals often involves aligning ourselves with priorities and principles not submitted to God. While many participants are unaware, these rites can invoke enemy spirits. Even if we've left the group, those agreements can remain binding until we renounce them. Repent of involvement in secret societies by you or your ancestors.

Renounce: "Demons and evil spirits, I renounce any involvement in Freemasonry and all secret societies. I break all agreements that I or my ancestors made with you. Your hold over me and my family ends now."

Repent: "Lord Jesus, please forgive me and my family for any involvement, known or unknown, with Freemasonry or any secret society."

5. Excessive Substance Abuse

Excessively using alcohol or drugs to the point of losing control, blacking out, or altering our state of consciousness destructively surrenders our self-control. The Bible is clear that drunkenness is a sin[3] and that we are to remain sober and alert.[4] Substance abuse not only harms our bodies, it provides a foothold for the enemy to influence us.

Renounce: "Demons and evil spirits, I break any agreement that I made with you while under the influence of drugs or alcohol."

Repent: "Lord Jesus, I repent of not staying in control of my faculties. Thank you for forgiving me."

6. Contemplating Suicide

Contemplating or planning to take our own life aligns us with the spirit of death, which Jesus came to destroy. When we agree with the lie that death is better than life, we're elevating the enemy above God, who alone determines our days.[5] If you've seriously considered suicide, renounce the spirit of death and break its hold over your mind.

Renounce: "Demons and evil spirits, I break any agreement that I made with you while contemplating suicide. I renounce any partnership with the spirit of death. Any consent I have given you is canceled."

Repent: "Lord Jesus, I repent of contemplating suicide. I repent of trying to play god. You, and You alone, will determine my days. Thank you for forgiving me."

7. Abuse

Enduring sexual, physical, or emotional abuse can drive victims to make inner vows like, "I will never let anyone hurt me again," or "I'll never trust anyone." While these self-protective promises are understandable, they grant the enemy access because they conflict with God's ways of forgiveness and trust. If you've suffered abuse, bring those wounds to Jesus for healing and cancel any destructive vows.

Renounce: "Demons and evil spirits, I break any agreement that I made with you while suffering abuse. Any consent I have given you is canceled."

Repent: "Lord Jesus, I repent of any agreement I made with the enemy while suffering abuse. I receive your healing from those wounds now in Jesus' name."

8. Envy and Selfish Ambition

James 3:16 warns that where envy and self-seeking exist, confusion and evil will exist. When we harbor jealousy toward others or use unscrupulous means to promote ourselves, we align with the enemy's methods and open doors to his influence in our endeavors and relationships. Renounce any envy or selfish ambition.

Renounce: "Demons and evil spirits, I renounce envy and selfish ambition. Any consent I have given you through envy or selfish ambition is now canceled. I break envy and selfish ambition in my life."

Repent: "Lord Jesus, I repent for being envious and self-seeking. Thank you for forgiving me."

9. Deception

One subtle doorway the enemy exploits is deception, such as faking an illness or misusing a weakness to avoid responsibility or gain sympathy. While not blatantly immoral, this dishonesty grieves the Spirit of truth and permits the father of lies to operate. God wants us to walk with complete integrity. Repent of any falsehood or exaggeration.

Renounce: "Demons and evil spirits, I break any agreement I made with you while attempting to deceive others. I cancel all agreements I made with you."

Repent: "Lord Jesus, I repent of deception to avoid responsibility or gain sympathy. Thank you for forgiving me. I receive your healing for me now, in Jesus' name."

10. Word Curses

The Bible teaches that life and death are in the power of the tongue.[6] When we speak negatively about ourselves, like "I'm so stupid," or receive curses from others, like "You'll never amount to anything," we agree with the enemy's slander. Those word curses can take root and shape our lives. Break the power of negative words by renouncing them and declaring God's truth instead.

Renounce: "Demons and evil spirits, I renounce any words spoken to myself or received from others that do not agree with God's Word. I renounce any negative self-talk. Any consent I have given you through word curses is now canceled. I break all word curses on my life, in Jesus' name."

Repent: "Lord Jesus, I repent of speaking or receiving words that are not in accordance with your will. I repent of all negative self-talk and of receiving negativity from others. Thank you for forgiving me."

11. Generational Curses

Scripture teaches that the sin patterns of our ancestors can be passed down through family lines.[7] While we are not guilty of their choices, the enemy often claims access through any area they gave him. Typical generational strongholds include addiction, sexual immorality, pride, anger, and fear. Renounce and cut off these inherited tendencies in Jesus' name.

Renounce: "Demons and evil spirits, I break the generational curses of (*fill in the blank*)... I break them from my mother's side, and I break them from my father's side. Your hold over me and my family ends today."

Repent: "Lord Jesus, I repent of any participation in generational curses. Thank you for forgiving me."

Making a Clean Sweep

After thoroughly examining our lives and closing every door we are aware of, a final step of deliverance is beneficial. In the authority of Jesus' name, command any remaining enemy strongholds to leave:

"In the mighty name of Jesus, I command any unclean spirits that have been oppressing me to go now. I have renounced your access and repented for my sin. You no longer have any legal right to remain. I break your power over my life and expel you completely. Leave me now and never return.

As children of God, we have been given the authority to resist the devil and watch him flee.[8] The more confidently we exercise this authority, the more we experience peace, hope, and joy. Remember, Jesus came to destroy the devil's works[9] and set captives free.[10]

Walking in Victory

Identifying and closing open doors is a pivotal step in our spiritual growth, but it's not the end of the journey. As we continue pursuing intimacy with Jesus and obeying His word, the Holy Spirit will likely reveal additional areas that need addressing. The goal is not perfection but rather a consistent habit of keeping short accounts with God - quickly recognizing and repenting of any footholds we've given the enemy.

We must also learn to stand firm in Christ's triumph on our behalf. When the enemy tries to regain access through deception, temptation, accusation, or intimidation, we must wield the truth of our identity in Christ and the power of His blood. Daily renewing our minds with Scripture, wearing the armor of God, and abiding in prayerful dependence are essential weapons for maintaining the freedom Jesus has won.

As we experience greater liberation from enemy influences, God often opens doors to minister that same freedom to others. Just as Jesus set us free so we could free others,[11] we have the privilege of sharing the keys of deliverance with those who are struggling. The Body of Christ will be transformed as more and more believers learn to recognize open doors and assert their God-given authority.

I pray that you will walk in the fullness of freedom Jesus purchased for you, closing every door to the enemy and living in the spacious place of God's blessing and purpose. As the Apostle Paul exhorted, "It is for freedom that Christ has set us free. Stand firm, then, and do not let yourselves be burdened again by a yoke of slavery" (Galatians 5:1 NIV). May you step boldly into the glorious liberty as a child of God!

---

[1] 1 John 1:9

[2] Deuteronomy 18:10-12

[3] Ephesians 5:18

[4] 1 Peter 5:8

[5] Psalm 139:16

[6] Proverbs 18:21

[7] Exodus 20:5

[8] James 4:7

[9] 1 John 3:8

[10] Luke 4:18

[11] Matthew 10:8

Mike Manuel

Chapter 12

Hearing From Jesus

As we conclude our journey of breaking up with the enemy, I want to share a vital truth: This process is not ultimately about the enemy; it's about Jesus. While we have necessarily focused on recognizing and renouncing the devil's schemes, our goal is not to become preoccupied with spiritual warfare but to clear the way for deeper intimacy with Jesus.

In this final exercise, we will intentionally create space to encounter Jesus personally. He desires to speak to you, encourage you, and reveal Himself to you in a fresh way. Scripture assures us that He will draw near to us if we draw near to Him.[1] Jesus promised, "The one who loves me will be loved by my Father, and I too will love them and *show myself to them*" (John 14:21 NIV). God also promised, "You will seek me and find me when you seek me with all your heart." (Jeremiah 29:13 NIV)

Here are some steps to help you posture your heart and hear from Jesus:

1. Find a quiet, comfortable place to be alone and undistracted. This may mean turning off your phone, dimming the lights, or lying down. Create an environment conducive to focusing on the Lord. Consider playing some worship music to help you come into a place of appreciation for the Lord.

2. Close your eyes and shift your attention from the natural to the spiritual realm. Ask the Holy Spirit to heighten your spiritual senses and tune your heart to His frequency.

3. Fix your thoughts on Jesus. Meditate on His character, His promises, and His presence with you. If it helps, recall a favorite image or description of Jesus from Scripture or picture Him beside you.

4. As you feel His presence, start your conversation with Him by asking, "Jesus, what do You like best about me?" Take time to listen for His response. Jesus often speaks to us through the "still, small voice" of the Holy Spirit in our hearts.[2]

5. Another great question that Jesus would probably love to answer for you is this: "Jesus,

what do You know about me that I don't know about me?" Again, take time to hear His answer. He may speak to your spirit or show you a word picture.

6. If Jesus invites you to a specific place in the Spirit, follow His lead. He may want to show you something, give you a vision, or simply commune with you. Trust His guidance and enjoy His presence.

7. Before concluding, ask Jesus this question: "Jesus, is there anything else You want to tell me or show me?" Again, give plenty of time for His answer.

8. Take a moment to thank Jesus for His love and willingness to fellowship with you. Ask Him to continue speaking to you and helping you abide in His presence daily.

Remember, encountering Jesus should not be a one-time event but a lifelong journey. As you practice listening for His voice and seeking His face, your relationship with Him will grow more quickly than you might imagine. Always remember that He delights in revealing Himself to His children.

May this meeting with Jesus be a launching point into a life of ever-deepening intimacy with Him. As you walk out your freedom in the days ahead, keep pursuing the One whose power and love sets you free.

---

[1] James 4:8

[2] 1 Kings 19:12

Epilogue

Living in Freedom

As we conclude this journey of breaking up with the enemy, I want to pause and celebrate the profound work God has done in your life. If you have fully engaged in this process—renouncing the enemy's influence, repenting before God, and closing every open door—I am confident you are already experiencing a tangible difference. The weights that once hindered you have been lifted, and you are tasting the freedom Jesus purchased for you.

While this book has necessarily focused on recognizing and evicting the enemy's work, I encourage you, as you move forward, to fix your eyes on Jesus, the Author and Perfecter of your faith.[1] He is the One who sets us free, and in His presence, we find the fullness of life. As you abide in Him, walking in obedience to His word and surrendering to His Spirit, you will continue to experience greater freedom and transformation.

However, we must remember that our adversary is persistent. Stay alert to his schemes as you rejoice in your liberation. If you do find yourself slipping back into old patterns or opening new doors to the enemy, don't despair. You now have the tools to shut those doors as quickly as they open. Recognize the access point, renounce it, repent before God, and reassert your authority in Christ. The more consistently you do this, the more impenetrable your defenses against the enemy will become.

Your capacity to advance God's Kingdom increases as you learn to live from a place of victory. No longer preoccupied with your bondage, you will have greater clarity, energy, and boldness to serve others and share the Gospel. Your freedom is not just for your benefit but for the blessing of the people around you.

To that end, I encourage you to share this book with others. Don't keep the keys of freedom to yourself! Invite your family, friends, and fellow believers to read this book. Offer to walk alongside them, praying for them and holding them accountable. As more and more Christians learn to live in the liberty Christ died to give us, the Church will be transformed, and the enemy's kingdom will suffer devastating losses.

My prayer for you is that you will encounter the depths of God's love in unprecedented ways in the days and years ahead. May His grace empower you to walk in holiness, humility, and unbroken fellowship with Him. And may He use your freedom to bring many others into His glorious light.

Thank you for participating in this journey of breaking up with the enemy. I am honored to have played a small part in God's great work in your life. Press on in your pursuit of Jesus because the best is yet to come!

And I am certain that God, who began the good work within you, will continue his work until it is finally finished on the day when Christ Jesus returns.

Philippians 1:6 NLT

---

[1] Hebrews 12:2

A Note from the Author,

Thank you for taking the time to read this book. If you have benefitted from what you've read or feel that others would benefit from reading this, please leave a review by using this QR code. Your review helps make this book more visible online so that others can benefit from it as well. Thank you so much for your review!

For more resources, visit my website at www.MikeManuel.faith

- Mike

Made in the USA
Coppell, TX
24 February 2026

72277793R00085